PINK AND Blue

Telling the Boys from the Girls in America

JO B. PAOLETTI

INDIANA UNIVERSITY PRESS

Bloomington and Indianapolis

This book is a publication of

Indiana University Press
601 North Morton Street
Bloomington, Indiana 47404-3797 USA

iupress.indiana.edu

Telephone orders 800-842-6796
Fax orders 812-855-7931

⊖ The paper used in this publication
meets the minimum requirements of
the American National Standard for
Information Sciences—Permanence
of Paper for Printed Library Materials,
ANSI Z39.48-1992.

Manufactured in the United States of
America

Library of Congress Cataloging-in-
Publication Data

Paoletti, Jo Barraclough, [date]
  Pink and blue : telling the boys from
the girls in America / Jo B. Paoletti.
  p. cm.
  Includes bibliographical references and
index.
  ISBN 978-0-253-00117-7 (cloth : alk.
paper) — ISBN 978-0-253-00130-6
(e-book) 1. Boys' clothing—United
States—History. 2. Girls' clothing—
United States—History. 3. Clothing and
dress—United States—Sex differences.
I. Title.
  TT630.P36 2012
  646'.30973—dc23
                              2011039889

       1 2 3 4 5 17 16 15 14 13 12

To Jim,
Maria, and
Danny,

with all my love

CONTENTS

ACKNOWLEDGMENTS

IT HAS TAKEN ME OVER TWENTY YEARS to write this book and thirty years to do the research. This is not boasting; it is a humble admission of my own tendencies to distraction and procrastination, aggravated by the normal vicissitudes of motherhood and scholarly life. There have been false starts, dead ends, and so many bouts of writer's block that not writing became my normal habit. There would still be no book if it weren't for the help, inspiration, and encouragement of family, friends, and colleagues who have never let this project disappear from my imagination.

Professional organizations are the heart of any discipline, but especially for a nomad like me. I would like to thank the Costume Society of America and the Association of College Professors of Textiles and Clothing (now the International Textiles and Apparel Association) for welcoming me as a graduate student, mentoring me as a scholar, and giving me a supportive but critical environment to publish and present my work. The lively community and fresh ideas of the Popular Culture Association, especially the Fashion and Appearance area, under the leadership of Joe Hancock of Drexel University, have also nourished me. The Material Culture Caucus of the American Studies Association helped me adjust to a new research paradigm when the dissolution of the University of Maryland's Textiles and Consumer Economics Department resulted in my migration to American Studies.

For involving me in projects that helped keep me out of the doldrums, I am grateful to Colleen Callahan, Claudia Kidwell, Carol Kregloh, Kate Rowland, and Valerie Steele. Michael Kimmel and Grant McCracken gave valuable feedback on an early paper that eventually grew into this book. Peggy Orenstein revived this project with a lengthy interview for a *New York Times Magazine* article about Disney Princesses that caused me to shake off my doubts and get back to work.

This research would not have been possible without access to archives and collections. I am indebted to the staff at the Winterthur Museum and

Library, especially Kay Collins of Academic Programs, who facilitated my stay as a visiting scholar, and Jeanne Solensky, Associate Librarian, Joseph Downs Collection of Manuscripts and Printed Ephemera. Patricia Hogan, curator of Toys and Dolls, Strong National Museum of Play, facilitated my use of their marvelous collection of paper dolls. Andrea Hughes, Curator of American Collections at the Children's Museum of Indianapolis, took time from her very busy schedule to help me examine items in multiple collections: garments, magazines, photographs, and more paper dolls. Mary Jane Teeters-Eichacker, Curator of Social History at the Indiana State Museum, not only opened the museum's costume collection to me but has followed up with additional "finds" she has encountered in her own research.

Russell A. Johnson of the History and Special Collections for the Sciences of the Louise M. Darling Biomedical Library at UCLA deserves special thanks for having the visionary idea that a collection of baby books might be of interest to researchers. His warm and enthusiastic response to my initial query resulted in my applying for a James and Sylvia Thayer Short-Term Research Fellowship. The fellowship made it possible for me to travel across the country and access this unique collection.

My University of Maryland colleagues John Caughey, Christina Hanhardt, R. Gordon Kelly, Katie King, Jeffrey McCune, Sheri Parks, Eden Segal, Mary Sies, Nancy Struna, and Psyche Williams-Forson provided moral support and collegial conversations. Reference librarians are worth their weight in gold; I can never adequately thank Barbara Wurtzel for her long-distance (and long-term!) research help and Eric Lindquist for helping me keep my research tool kit up-to-date. I owe an enormous debt of gratitude to Jane Behnken, Sarah Wyatt Swanson, Raina Polivka, and June Silay of Indiana University Press, who provided support and guidance throughout the long book-birthing process. Copyeditor Elaine Otto snipped, tightened, and smoothed my manuscript with diligence and humor. In addition, I have benefited from the editing efforts of Renee Lagrid and Marybeth Shea. Marybeth has also been a steadfast source of questions, photographs, and company.

Finally, I must give loving thanks to my family. Jim, my patient husband of over forty years, has encouraged my work and made it possible by taking on laundry, grocery shopping, and cooking without being asked. At this point, he knows when I am in a writing groove and when it's time for a beer. Our children, Maria (b. 1982) and Danny (b. 1986), didn't set out to inspire my research, nor did I take on parenthood in order to find a new area of inquiry. But the universe brought them into my life at exactly the right time, and I am grateful for their willingness to let me observe their childhood so closely.

INTRODUCTION

THIS JOURNEY BEGAN NEARLY THIRTY YEARS AGO with a deceptively simple question: When did we start dressing girls in pink and boys in blue? As it turned out, the complexity of this topic is astonishing, extending far beyond the color of blankets and booties. The visual vocabulary seems endless: pink and blue, ruffles and neckties, lace and camouflage, kittens and lions, butterflies and airplanes. Gender symbolism in American children's fashions is ubiquitous. It is also transmitted clearly enough that most children know these unwritten rules thoroughly by the age of three. This might lead to the assumption that the rules have changed little over time, but the opposite is true. In little more than a century, the rules have changed so dramatically that the conventions of 2010 are nearly the reverse of those in 1890.

This book is an attempt to describe and explain some of the most evident of those changes, to settle some popular questions about the rationale and effect of gendered clothing on children, and to clear a path for future research. I am excruciatingly aware that you, my readers, may be dress historians, scholars or students from some other field (ranging from gender studies to neurobiology), or interested parents or grandparents. There is no way to satisfy everyone, so I hope that you will forgive me if I seem to be too academic, not theoretical enough, or I describe clothing in too much detail. As long as we continue to grapple with questions about the nature and origin of gender differences, it will be important for researchers to communicate their findings in accessible language. My intention is to write clearly and to cite thoroughly, which I hope will satisfy readers across the spectrum.

It should be evident that this book is an initial foray into the topic and cannot be about American children in all of their diversity. As is the case with much of fashion history, the artifactual and printed record is skewed toward middle- and upper-class consumers. My primary evidence is drawn from a wide variety of sources:

- Advice manuals and childcare literature, in the form of books and articles in popular magazines
- Retail catalogs, especially Sears, Roebuck & Co.
- Advertisements and articles in fashion magazines and newspapers
- Photographs in public and private collections
- Paper dolls published in newspapers, magazines, and booklets
- Baby record books
- Surviving examples of children's clothing in public and private collections
- Trade publications for the garment industry, especially *Earnshaw's Infants, Girls and Boys Wear Review*
- Comments posted on blogs, news articles, and online social networks.

Each of these sources provides a generous—even overwhelming—amount of evidence, but all are much less informative about the influence of race, class, religion, or region on clothing options and choices. Until the 1960s, only white children were depicted in most clothing advertising and catalogs. Even in the baby books, which were filled out for a specific child, the child's race was not apparent unless the record included photographs, a copy of the birth certificate, or similar evidence. Only one of the eight hundred baby books I examined at the UCLA library clearly belonged to an African American child. Ethnicity and religion could sometimes be deduced from surnames and other information, but not frequently enough to discern a pattern. Similarly, it appears likely that there have always been regional variations in how children are dressed, but the national sources seldom offer such a nuanced view. I have tried to include images of children of other races whenever possible and to include a sense of which variations and patterns are supported by the evidence. However, since my primary intention in this book has been to explain "the rules" as they were articulated in popular culture, the interesting question of how the rules were followed (or not) by different groups of Americans must be left for another time or another researcher.

In the interest of readability, the use of qualifying phrases has been minimized; when I refer to "mothers and fathers," it is with the understanding that such generalizations include other caregivers. I hope that other researchers will rise to the challenges evident in this very limited beginning.

My particular viewpoint on the history and meaning of gender differences in children's clothing has been formed not only by my own primary research but also by several theoretical strands. The most useful have been material culture studies, history of childhood, consumer culture, developmental psychology, and the psychology of dress. This introduction explains my approach to material culture studies and the scope and nature of my research. The next chapter provides some background for understanding the material evidence, using the theoretical contributions of the other fields, and my own emerging theory of the generational element in fashion change.

MATERIAL CULTURE STUDIES

Material culture involves those tangible aspects of the human experience that are created or modified by humans. Clothing is material culture, as are tools, cities, food, and hundreds of thousands of artifacts, or objects, large and small. Archaeologists, art historians, anthropologists, and popular culture scholars all study material culture, and the public encounters the results of their work in places as diverse as Colonial Williamsburg and the PBS show *Antiques Roadshow*. Material culture scholarship may be used in conjunction with other research methods and theoretical constructs, from metallurgy to postmodernism, but most material culture studies have one thing in common: artifacts. Every type of artifact imposes certain requirements on the scholar. To study clothing, one must understand how it is made, the materials used, how it is produced and distributed, how it is worn and cared for, in order to interpret its historical importance or cultural meaning. My education and training is in apparel design and textiles, and it included coursework in textile science, the history of clothing and textiles, and the economics of the textile and garment industries. This multidisciplinary perspective informed my analysis of actual clothing, visual representations of children's fashions (photographs, ads, paper dolls), and written accounts and descriptions.

It is not uncommon for several types of material objects to be used to study another, as is the case with this research, which interprets the meaning of children's clothing through three artifactual sources: garments, paper dolls, and baby books. These other sources were vital because even the best museum collection does not represent the typical or everyday as much as it does the precious or the unusual. Examining museum objects is unparalleled for understanding design and construction at a level of detail impossible from other sources, but it cannot be the basis for generalizing about what "most children" wore at a given time. If we relied on historic dress collections alone, we would conclude that there were about five times as many girls as boys, that they spent half of their lives at parties, hardly ever slept, and never got dirty.

Paper dolls proved to be an invaluable resource. These popular playthings are now prized collectibles, meaning that there is a wealth of information about their history and manufacture to assist with their interpretation. Telling the boys from the girls and discerning the age of the child was usually a simple affair, since most commercial paper dolls were labeled with the characters' names and ages. The dolls' wardrobes included outfits for many activities, both formal and informal, sleepwear and accessories, and even underwear (usually on the doll itself). Best of all for my purposes, families of dolls were common, with brothers and sisters and even brother-sister twins wearing "girl" and "boy" versions of the same design.

Perhaps the most exciting find of the project was the collection of baby books at the UCLA Louise Darling Biomedical Library's History and Special Collections unit. This unique collection of over 1,300 "memory books" dating from the late nineteenth century to the present actually straddles two categories: manuscript sources and material objects. The books contain not only handwritten records for individual children but also baby bracelets, fabric swatches, locks of hair, and other mementos. Birth announcements and greeting cards were also preserved in the books, adding another dimension to the history of pink and blue color coding. Most baby books also included information about the family's location, making them my best source about regional variations.

OVERVIEW: HOW THE NARRATIVE IS ORGANIZED

The organization of this book is roughly chronological, but it consists of several overlapping and interconnected narratives, separated into distinct chapters. Gendered clothing for babies and young children didn't burst, full-blown, on the American market, nor did it evolve at the same rate for infants and toddlers or boys and girls. The definitions of "baby" and "child" have changed over time, and the age at which the infant no longer wears baby clothes has also changed since the late nineteenth century. Sometimes I have been able to interpret style changes in the context of current findings and theories from gender acquisition research, but when it didn't make sense, I have not. Those theories are summarized in chapter 1, so readers have access to them from the beginning and should feel free to draw their own conclusions.

Chapter 2, "Dresses Are for Girls and Boys," will focus on the convention of putting both little boys and girls in dresses, which was the accepted practice in Europe and America through the early years of the twentieth century. The significance of white dresses for babies and toddlers will be discussed, as well as their transformation into the ceremonial christening gown. This occurred within the context of the transition from a view of babies as sexless cherubs to a view of babies as nascent men and women. Gradually, dresses were reclassified as feminine, rather than neutral, and replaced by rompers, knitted sleepers, and "onesies" (combination undershirt and diaper cover).

Chapter 3, "Pants Are for Boys and Girls," follows the transformation of a formerly masculine class of garments—pants and other bifurcated styles—into a neutral garment that could be gendered by varying cut, color, or decoration. The masculinization of boys' clothing paralleled and influenced the modernization of girls' clothing, which involved adopting styles that were shorter, plainer, and—most significant—featured pants or shorts for active wear. Had the transformation that occurred in boys' clothing happened thirty years earlier, toddler boys might have had exclusive use of pants for a generation before their adoption by girls. This might have prevented or delayed the acceptance of trousers for girls. Instead, the convergence of these two trends—younger boys wearing trousers instead of dresses and girls wearing rompers and overalls—initiated a long process of developing feminized designs that could be distinguished from pants for boys. This, in turn, helped to clarify the visual lexicon of feminine details for all clothing items

The first two chapters detail the rearrangement of neutral clothing options, a change that forms the backdrop for the development of exclusively masculine and feminine styles. The gendering process for boys' and girls' clothing was neither evenhanded nor simultaneous, however.

Chapter 4, "A Boy Is Not a Girl," traces the transition from ungendered to gendered clothing for toddlers and children between 1900 and 1930, which was primarily focused on boys' fashions. During this time, little boys' fashions gradually acquired more elements of adult male dress, while details once considered neutral and "youthful"—including flowers, dainty trim, and the color pink—were relegated to girls and women. The process of adding some colors, cuts, and details and subtracting (and redefining) others takes place at varying speeds—rapidly between 1900 and 1910, 1940 and 1950, and 1980 and 1990, with periods of slower change in between. The first shift coincides with the coming of age of boys who wore Little Lord Fauntleroy suits in the 1880s and 1890s, which suggests a generational explanation. The rejection of feminine styling for boys and the reclassification of formerly neutral elements as feminine may also be attributed to changing beliefs about sexuality and intensified anxiety about male homosexuality.

In chapter 5, "Pink Is for Boys," I detail the complex history of our most visible gender markers for babies. From the introduction of pink and blue as nursery colors, to their gradual acceptance as feminine and masculine hues, to today's ubiquitous use of pink as a sign of femininity, the complicated story provides insight into the deep changes in adult attitudes toward children's gender and sexuality. Sources from the early twentieth century prove that there was little agreement among manufacturers, retailers, or consumers on which color was feminine and which was masculine or whether they denoted gender at all. Part of the confusion stems from these new colors having been introduced from different places at around the same time, and the culturally diverse nature of America, since so many immigrants were arriving from southern and eastern Europe, where infant clothing traditions were quite different. Most of the confusion, however, can be attributed to the arbitrary nature of the assigned symbolism, no matter how natural it might seem to modern consumers.

Unisex clothing, discussed in chapter 6, appeared during a twenty-year hiatus in the steady genderizing of children's clothing, from roughly 1965 to 1985, ushered in by the confluence of the women's movement and the first baby boomers becoming parents. Popular critiques of traditional gender roles and scientific studies of gendered behaviors and identities argued for a characterization of femininity and masculinity as learned, culturally constructed behaviors—nurture, not nature. A steady stream of popular culture, from gender-bending youth fashions to children's books and music, broadcast the new ideal of unisex child rearing. Second-wave feminists took aim at feminine styles as undermining girls' development and access to power. This accounted for unisex styling not actually being neutral but mainly a matter of feminine details being replaced by masculine styling. The end of unisex clothing, in the mid-1980s, was marked by the introduction of Luvs diapers for girls (pink) and boys (blue). Since 1985, boys' clothing has changed little compared with styles for little girls, which have become frillier and pinker, with fewer tailored or plain options. I will argue that this paralleled the rise of third-wave feminism and a popular swing toward embracing biological determinism.

Chapter 7 examines the years since the mid-1980s, as neutral clothing has become scarce and strongly gendered clothing has become the norm. Department and specialty stores offer only a few ungendered options, usually limited to infants' sizes 0–24 months. While this trend has been enabled by prenatal testing and imaging that reveals the sex of the baby, it also reflects a strong desire on the part of the parents to make the child's gender clear to all onlookers and a popular embrace of essentialist views of femininity and masculinity. These trends also expose parental ambivalence and anxieties about their children's sexuality, whether their daughters' precocity and loss of innocence or their sons' careful navigation of the straits of masculinity, between violence and aggression on one extreme and effeminacy on the other. I will conclude with some observations on recent trends that suggest the end of the Reign of Pink, increasing consumer demand for neutral styles, and greater visibility of gender-variant children.

UNDERSTANDING CHILDREN'S CLOTHING

WHAT IS THE PURPOSE OF CULTURAL patterns such as gender conventions in clothing? How do we explain their existence? Do they simply arise out of a need in an earlier time and then continue through mindless transmission? Do they stem from societal structures and conflicts, manifested as material objects and patterns of their use? Or are they responses to those social structures—the way we change them over time to suit our changing environment? Or can our material world be reduced to the embodiment of neural impulses, evolutionary biology, or unconscious fears and desires? Unlike older children, babies and toddlers have little choice in their clothing, which reflects the attitudes and beliefs of adults. Since children are known to acquire sex role stereotypes and begin to fit their own identities to these cultural norms during these first years of life, this is a particularly useful way to understand how gender norms are negotiated, expressed, learned, and changed. It is important that we understand that these supposed "traditions" are of recent vintage and that they represent the culmination of just over a century of dramatic change in what has been considered appropriate dress for infants and small children.

To that end, it is important to clarify the scope of this book and the meanings of a few basic terms. In academic literature, the words "sex" and "gender" have specific meanings that are usually conflated in popular usage. To the scholar, "gender" refers to "cultural differences between men and women, based on the biological difference between men and women."[1] "Sex" is used to denote those biological differences (male, female); "gender" is used for distinctions in role, appearance, and behavior that are cultural in origin, but stemming from an individual's sex (masculinity and femininity). In practice, these classifications are more complex; recent scholarship has begun to take into consideration the fact that biological sex is not binary (either-or), with 1 in 100 adults having genetic or physical attributes other than "standard" male or female, including as many as 1 in 1,500 babies whose genitalia is sufficiently atypical that a specialist is consulted.[2] If sex is not binary, then it follows that "gender," being based on sex, is not binary, either. Current gender studies scholars are operating with a much more complex and fluid notion of both "sex" and "gender" than is represented by those terms in everyday speech.

Since this is a book about everyday culture, the common meanings of these terms should be assumed; when I intend a more specialized academic or theoretical usage, it will be noted explicitly. "Gender differences" in children's clothing refers to elements that are classified as "masculine," "feminine," or "neutral," almost in a grammatical sense. "Gender identity" will mean personal congruence with existing norms of masculinity or femininity, including the possibility of being at odds with those norms.[3] The words "sex," "male," "female," "boy," and "girl," when referring to the apparent (or assigned) biological sex of the child, all have a biological basis but cultural meanings. This is reflected in the common usage of the word "gender" to refer to biological sex, and most of the time I will be using "sex" and "gender" interchangeably, clarifying a more precise meaning as necessary.

This is about the clothing of children up to the age of about six or seven, living in the United States from 1885 through 2011, when this book was completed. The age limit is important; children learn the patterns of gender-appropriate dress and apply them to the construction of their own identities during the first seven years of life. Focusing on this age group enabled me to formulate connections between the history of gender differences in dress and the body of behavioral science research on gender identity acquisition in early childhood. The developmental stages within that age limit have been known by many names, including newborn, infant, child, toddler, and preschooler, and the boundaries for those distinctions have changed over time. This complicates the description of the appropriate styles for each age; an 18-month-old would be considered an "infant" in 1885 and a "toddler" in 1935. For the sake of clarity, these shifts will be noted within each section.

HISTORY AND CULTURE OF CHILDHOOD

The artifactual sources would have been sufficient if my intention was only to describe the gendering of children's clothing in America.[4] Understanding the confusing and contradictory landscape of children's clothing requires connecting that narrative with the work of scholars in other fields, beginning with the history of childhood.

The social history of childhood as an academic field emerged in the 1960s with the publication of *Centuries of Childhood* by French social historian Philippe Ariès. Although many of his conclusions have been reconsidered or rejected by later scholars, his work is still significant for its groundbreaking attention to everyday life and for his persuasive argument that the doctrine of original sin and infant depravity began to give way to a more complex view of the child as an innocent, malleable being with a soul capable of corruption or salvation. This shift paved the way for sweeping changes in childcare, education, and material culture—not only clothing but toys and furniture as well.

Historian Linda Pollock, drawing on British and American diaries and autobiographies, critiqued Ariès's argument that childhood was "invented" in the early modern period and the contentions of other scholars that higher infant mortality rates before the seventeenth century resulted in adult indifference to or neglect of babies. Her book, *Forgotten Children: Parent-Child Relations from 1500 to 1900*, provided convincing evidence that babies and children were loved, valued, and mourned as earnestly in the past as they are today. Her use of personal diaries and autobiographies, in addition to advice literature, was also instrumental in making other scholars more skeptical about the uncritical use of published advice. Pollock pointed out that advice literature often had no connection to actual practice, though it might illuminate *desired* behavior. This has certainly been the case with fashion advice, whether for children or adults; studies of nineteenth-century advice for men's clothing and for brides in mourning indicated that the authors copied freely from each other (multiplying their perceived impact) but were often widely ignored.[5] Comparing advice literature with evidence from baby books helped trace both the experts' changing standards and consumers' acceptance or rejection of the rules.

The work of material culture scholar Karin Calvert drew upon Pollock's research and added extensive study of the clothing, toys, and other furnishings of American children, particularly in the colonial era and the early republic. In *Children in the House: The Material Culture of Early Childhood, 1600–1900*, Calvert connected the works of Ariès, Pollock, and others with a close study of objects to convincingly argue not only that children in early America were perceived as impressionable, valued members of the family but also that their physical surroundings were designed to shape their bodies and their souls.

The works of historians Joseph F. Kett, William Bridges, and Mary Lynn Stevens Heininger are invaluable for detailing the changes wrought upon middle-class American families by the Industrial Revolution and the American Civil War. Men's work moved beyond the home, leaving women and children in a "separate sphere" idealized as a refuge from worldly vices and pressures but also the place where children (especially boys) must be prepared for that very world. This paradox provides dramatic tension in raising boys and dressing them appropriately. While girls could be kept at home and sheltered from the demands of industrial and commercial pursuits, boys must—eventually—leave behind the comfort and safety of home and go into the world to make their own way. Much of the complicated history of boys' clothing in the nineteenth century can be attributed to ambivalence about when and how to transition boys from babyhood to boyhood to youth to manhood. Girls were perceived as moving more smoothly though the years before puberty, when they experienced "wrenching adolescence" as the end of their childhood and the beginning of their preparation for courtship and marriage.[6]

The influence of scientific discoveries on child rearing at the end of the nineteenth century was considerable. The writings of Charles Darwin on the evolution of species may not have won over the general public, but the idea of "the survival of the fittest" as applied to societal competition, success, and failure was quickly propagated in popular culture and public discourse. Equipping boys for life beyond the home took on the urgency of racial survival, in the face of increased immigration from southern and eastern Europe. G. Stanley Hall and other pioneer child psychologists added another source of anxiety: subconscious desires and fears, stemming from early childhood, which could manifest themselves in adulthood as neuroses and depravity. Meanwhile, leaders in the women's rights movement were advocating for more freedom for women and more education for girls, to open up opportunities for them beyond home and family. Early feminists wrote passionately against the rigidity of expected gender roles for boys (playful and free) and girls (nurturing and useful) and against the very idea of separate developmental theories for boys and girls.[7] The convergence of these trends at the end of the century—ambivalence about the industrialized future, anxiety about competition and survival, challenges to existing gender roles—resulted in changes in children's lives that are visible in their very appearance.

CHILDREN AND CONSUMERISM

It is no secret that children in America have been the targets of manufacturers, advertisers, and marketers since the early twentieth century. Within the larger fields of the history of childhood, marketing, sociology, and media studies, countless researchers have documented the growing importance of consumption by and for children and analyzed its impact on boys and girls. Three scholars in particular have informed me to an unusual extent: cultural anthropologist Grant McCracken, sociologist Daniel Thomas Cook, and cultural historian Gary Cross.

Grant McCracken has written extensively on material culture and meaning, including works on gender symbolism and on generational interactions. His interrogation of the semiotic argument for a "language of fashion" in *Culture and Consumption* (1988) resonated deeply with my own early research into masculinity in men's and boys' clothing and Susan Kaiser's work in symbolic interaction in clothing behavior. The application of linguistic concepts once used in cultural studies—vocabularies, discourse analysis, and the like—has never worked well for the study of fashion, though it persists in popular works. It was, at best, a useful theoretical platform from which to survey the complex landscape of design, production, marketing, purchase, use, and disposal of clothing. But my experience with primary sources such as actual garments and ephemera is that they impose a reality that challenges theory, especially metaphor masquerading as theory. As an anthropologist, McCracken knows the messiness of culture and the difficulty of reducing cultural patterns to grammatical constructs. Nothing represents this as well to me as the typical long white baby dress from any of the many small museums I have visited: unlabeled, undated, and undocumented. If we attempt to "read" the meaning of the garment using our own presentist lexicon, we will interpret it as a christening gown, probably for a girl. The more we understand about the complete history of the garment, including why it was preserved, the more we must let go of the idea of a simple language of fashion that can be used to analyze meaning beyond a particular specific context. McCracken also brings a keen sense of business to the study of

consumer culture, which is absolutely essential. There are too many otherwise valuable articles and books on the subject that rely almost entirely
on other articles about history, culture, and consumption but include
only a handful of industry or business sources.

Gary Cross's work on consumer culture in general and children's
toys in particular have not only provided parallel connections to my examination of clothing but have also set the standard for thorough, nuanced work in the field of consumer studies. His first major work, *Time
and Money: The Making of Consumerist Modernity* (1993), provided essential background in the technological, commercial, and demographic
changes that made modern American consumption possible. His works
on children's toys and amusements, *Kids' Stuff* (1999) and *The Cute and
the Cool* (2004), further illuminated the convergence of child-centered
educational theories, middle-class parental concerns about their children's future success, and psychology-driven advertising.

Children under the age of seven, the primary subjects of this book,
are not consumers in the usual sense. Their parents and other adults act
as their purchasing agents, acquiring goods and services on their behalf,
according to their own beliefs and values. To be sure, modern children
may have a more powerful voice in these decisions, but parents still hold
the purse strings or the credit card. Daniel Thomas Cook's study of *The
Commodification of Childhood* (2004) has explained this relationship, especially as it pertained to mothers in the first half of the twentieth century and interpreted this relationship in the context of the evolution of
the children's clothing industry through the early history of *The Infant's
Department* (now *Earnshaw's Review*). Particularly valuable are his insights into the invention of the "toddler" as a developmental stage and
a clothing size and the intertwined roles of the children's wear industry
and advice writers. The most significant changes in the gendering of children's clothing occurred within this emerging age range during the exact
period when the "toddler" was introduced. Moreover, they occurred just
as parents began to consult and value the opinions of small children in
making purchases for them, suggesting that the period between 1910 and
1930 marks the birth of the American "consumer-tot." Like Cross, Cook
recognized the important shift in the parents' role in children's consumption, from primary actors to *reactors* responding to children's desires.
Central to understanding children's commercial culture is the notion of
the "symbolic child," which is neither real nor ideal but a constructed

image of "the baby," "the toddler," "the boy," and "the girl."[8] It is for this symbolic child that clothing is designed and marketed, and the concept of the symbolic child is very useful for analyzing children's fashions as seen in catalogs, advertisements, and advice literature. Material culture analysis must play a part in the study of consumer culture because symbolic children don't wear real clothes, and artifacts have a way of complicating symbols.

CHILDREN AND GENDER IDENTITY

Historical context is vital to the study of material and culture, and it is comfortable territory for someone like myself, trained in artifact and documentary research. Venturing into the less familiar field of developmental psychology was a formidable challenge but, as it turns out, even more necessary. From the very beginning, one question consistently emerged from audiences or interviewers whenever I shared my research: "Does it matter what little children wear?" Of course, it was not always raised in those exact words. A fifth-grader might ask if the boy in the Little Lord Fauntleroy suit was a sissy; a teenager would ask if he turned out gay. Parents would share anecdotes about tree-climbing princesses, or they asked if they should be concerned if their sons clamored for nail polish. Begging off, with the excuse that I am a fashion historian, not a psychologist, might let me dodge the question temporarily, but it stuck in my mind and demanded an answer.

Another factor that led me to the psychological literature was a citation search on my own published works. A citation search begins with a book or article and locates other works that refer to, or cite, that publication. I was just looking to see what scholarship had been done in the general field of children's clothing and gender, and this was one way to approach the task. I expected to find works in children's history, fashion, and gender studies. I did not expect to learn that psychologists and neuroscientists, most of them studying some aspect of gender identity in small children, had also cited my work. Discovering this unknown audience for my research prompted me to learn more about what they were learning about this subject of mutual interest.

Any review of current literature leads the curious researcher back in time, through the history of that discipline. In the case of child development literature, tracing the path of theories about gender acquisition had a dual function. First, it helped me see which models had been discredited and discarded (such as early Freudian explanations about the origins of homosexuality and John Money's work on the malleability of gender identity in the case of intersex or surgically reassigned children)[9] and which had withstood clinical testing and had earned long-lasting acceptance. In this introduction, I will focus on those which have been useful in developing my own theories of the mechanism of fashion change, but in each chapter, where appropriate, I have incorporated the theories that appear to have influenced popular child care literature and parenting practices. These include the pre-psychology writings of Jean-Jacques Rousseau and John Locke, the work of G. Stanley Hall (sometimes called "the father of child psychology" and an influential advocate of gender-specific treatment of young children), and the many "Baby X" studies in the 1970s, which illuminated how a baby's assigned sex influenced strangers' responses to the child.

To answer the question of the impact that dress might have on children under six, I have turned to the literature in clothing and human behavior, including Sandra Lipsitz Bem's concept of gender schema and Eleanor Emmons Maccoby's social learning theory. The vast, interdisciplinary study of fashion as a social and cultural phenomenon encompasses the humanities, psychology, and sociology as well as anthropology and economics. Some of the earliest works still inform current scholars, including economist Thorstein Veblen's *Theory of the Leisure Class* (1899), which introduced the concept of conspicuous consumption, and sociologist Georg Simmel's 1904 essay "Fashion," which posited both a trickle-down mechanism for fashion adoption and the role of class and power differentials in maintaining the fashion system.

Despite the widespread misconception of fashion as superficial and devoid of larger cultural significance (not unlike the common image of popular culture in general), over a century of academic research on the topic tells otherwise.[10] Clothing has many practical purposes—protection and modesty are often posited as the earliest motivations—but the archeological record suggests that ancient people used clothing very much as we use it today: to express our individuality, our station in life, our availability for sex or marriage, and even our mood. Gender distinctions are among the oldest and most widespread functions of dress. Because of these performative functions, researchers in this field have referred to themselves as *costume* historians, confusing the general public, who associate the term with theater or Hallowe'en. This appellation has given way to *dress* or *fashion historian,* though it persists in the names of the major professional organizations in the United States and Great Britain. Still, to the scholar, all clothing—even the most practical—has an element of "playing the part."

Fashionable dress is a subcategory of clothing: styles that are popular or acceptable for a period of time by a particular social group. Fashion, by its very definition, is subject to change. Most historians date the modern form of fashion—rapid introduction and abandonment of trends, led by a powerful social class, and supported by an industry driven by novelty—to the fourteenth century in western Europe. Other consumer goods (cars, food, music) are subject to trends, but the association between clothing and fashion is so close and so old that the term "fashion industry" is synonymous with the design, production, and sale of garments.

Fashion participation is very much a matter of gender. Women are expected to be aware of fashion, and they buy most of the clothing, not only for themselves but also for men and children. Men used to be *very* engaged in fashion; wealthy merchants and nobles prior to the nineteenth century used the latest clothing to express their affluence and power. As Veblen and Simmel pointed out, responsibility for fashionable display shifted from men to women and children by the end of the nineteenth century, when my story begins. Clothing for children under three, in contrast, has not always been as fashion-driven as it is today. Throughout most of the nineteenth century, styles for babies and the youngest children changed more slowly and less radically compared with the dress of older children and women. Advice writers criticized mothers who devoted too much attention to fashion for this age group as either being wasteful or training their children to be vain. As Daniel Cook points out in *The Commodification of Childhood,* the industry's construction of the child consumer between 1910 and 1940 required recasting the style changes intrinsic to fashion as a moral good—something that was beneficial for a child's well-being. Fashionable clothing became a means of fitting in and instilling self-confidence, even in very young children.

The psychological study of clothing has almost as long a history as the field of psychology itself, beginning with *The Psychology of Clothing* by George V. Dearborn (1918) and *The Psychology of Fashion* by J. C. Flugel (1930). Among Dearborn's arguments was the idea that the sensation of being well-dressed was "statable scientifically" as "relief and protection from various kinds of fears" and men and boys were particularly motivated by the power of subconscious fear. Flugel applied the methods and theories of psychoanalysis to the differences between men's and women's dress and came to the conclusion that women's clothing—having been recently modernized in the 1920s—was evolving faster and advancing further than that of men, who were held back by their subconscious fears of ridicule and loss of power. Many in the psychoanalytical school of clothing research saw sexual "deviance"—including homosexuality, transvestism, and masturbation (all of which they often conflated)—as the result of inadequate identification with the opposite-sex parent and narcissistic tendencies.

Most of the clothing behavior research focused on adults, not children, until the 1960s, when interest in sex role acquisition was stimulated by the social questions stirred up by the women's liberation movement. Jeanne Brooks-Gunn listed the three main theoretical schools of the time, each arguing for a particular dominant mechanism:

- Identification (influenced by Freudian psychology): the child learns gender roles by imitating an adult model to whom he or she is attached emotionally.
- Cognitive development (Piaget): the child is the agent of his own identity, through a process of learning and enacting gender rules.
- Social learning: the child learns gender rules socially, through a process of reward and punishment.[11]

Psychologist and women's studies scholar Sandra Lipsitz Bem, in a 1983 article in the interdisciplinary feminist journal *Signs,* argued for a "gender schema" model that combined the cognitive development and social learning theories. In the gender schema model, the child constructs gender identity by processing messages from social community and fitting them together with previously received information. This is conceived to be a lifelong process; adults continue to acquire new information and adjust their gender identities accordingly. Cultural associations of gender—stereotypes—play an important early role in this process, but not necessarily a permanent role. As children mature, they are able to better understand the nuances and variations of human behavior and therefore are capable of rejecting stereotypes as "required" behavior. Her own empirical studies suggested that adults whose identities exhibit a strong gender schema tend to perpetuate and rely on gender stereotypes, while "gender aschematic" individuals seemed less informed by stereotypes when assessing the behavior and appearance of others.[12]

The concept of gender schema is very useful to the study of clothing, as it aptly describes the stereotypical elements found in dress. Its major drawback is that, as this book demonstrates, those elements are not static but fluid. The appropriate expressions of masculinity and femininity, like the characteristics they signify, are not clear-cut, and this ambiguity helps drive change. Social learning theory of gender acquisition, combined with interactionism (also called social interactionism), provides the necessary framework for studying gender symbolism within a dynamic system such as fashion. The works of Eleanor Emmons Maccoby and Susan B. Kaiser have been particularly useful in my own research.

Maccoby is associated with both social learning theory and interactionism applied to the study of sex differences in children's behavior and their acquisition of gender identity. Maccoby has always argued that gender roles are both biological and cultural in origin, shaped by social interactions. In this equation, she assigns the most weight to social interactions, and much of her research concerns the relative importance of a child's interactions with peers, parents, and siblings.[13] For my purposes, Maccoby's most salient discoveries are found in her 1998 book, *The Two Sexes: Growing Up Apart, Coming Together,* which focuses on children's play and choice of playmates, but offers the following insights that have implications for how clothing is used to construct gender identity: "Children begin to understand clusters of sequences of gendered objects and actions [building blocks of what Sandra Bem labeled 'gender schema'] in infancy and early childhood. The cognitive process of creating meaning from concrete experiences is still unknown."[14]

She notes that "3-year-olds know their own gender, and know which toys are for boys and girls, but don't always use those rules, especially when playing alone." She adds that "4-year-olds make consistent sex-typed choices and are usually positive about them. From 4 to about 8, gender appropriate behaviors are a moral imperative."[15]

Maccoby believes that "mothers and fathers behave differently as 'agents' of sex-typing. Fathers are more likely to treat sons and daughters according to gender schema; mothers respond more to their children's needs that are the result of immaturity than to their needs as boys or girls."[16] She also cites researchers who have contributed to our understanding of the social learning of gender. In particular, M. B. Boston and G. D. Levy indicated that preschool girls understand both male and female scripts (schema or sets of rules), while boys understand male scripts better than they do female scripts.[17] I would suggest that this might be either because male rules are a "prerequisite" for learning the female rules (and boys have no compelling reason to learn "girls' rules") or because some of the boys' rules are actually girls' rules restated as negatives (NOT pink, NOT a dress, and so on). The work of Judith Harris on group socialization theory has been particularly persuasive that children socialize each other, using cultural information learned from adults.[18] Together with Maccoby's findings on play patterns, this suggests that other children, especially same-sex peers, act as "enforcers" of gender rules. Children aged four to five years, according to Maccoby, play mostly with their own sex (excluding siblings) not only in the United States but in Africa, India, Mexico, and the Philippines as well.

The influence of symbolic interaction theory on clothing studies dates back to the work of social psychologists in the 1960s, particularly Gregory Stone's "Appearance and the Self" (originally published in 1962 and widely reprinted) and Herbert Blumer's "Fashion: From Class Differentiation to Collective Selection." Symbolic interaction (or interactionism, as it is sometimes called) involves qualitative study of the processes by which individuals use elements of their cultural environment to construct identity through social interactions. Many clothing behavior researchers have found this a useful approach for the study of children's' use of clothing to construct gender identity, a field dominated by the works of Susan B. Kaiser. Like Eleanor Maccoby, Kaiser sees both cognitive and social learning at work in children's choices, and her recent theoretical work has emphasized the importance of ambiguity and anxiety as motivators for children's fashion changes. Kaiser found that girls over the age of five demonstrated "a decreased need for the sex-role reinforcement provided by dresses, and greater tolerance of gender ambiguity."[19] This suggests that as children mature, they learn that gender is permanent and not subject to change based simply on a change in appearance, making them less dependent on stereotypical styles to support their identities. Kaiser and Kathleen Huun, in "Fashioning Innocence and Anxiety: Clothing, Gender, and Symbolic Childhood," argue that children's clothing fashion changes are shaped by anxieties about sexuality, which is observed very differently in girls (heterosexual loss of innocence) and in boys (homophobia and fear of effeminacy).

In addition to decades of research and theoretical development about the process of gender role identification, there is a valuable body of work, mostly dating to the late 1970s, which clearly established that adults interact with infants based on their assumed sex, talking more to "girls" and engaging more in physical play with "boys." Together with the interactionist and other research into how slightly older children use these and other environment clues to construct their understanding and performance of gender, we have some idea of the role played in the process by clothing. In infancy, clothing shapes the response of others to the baby. Once children learn gender terms ("boy," "man," "girl," "woman," and even "mama" and "dada"), they begin to connect those terms to other pieces of the puzzle, including clothing. They learn to correctly assign gender using hair and clothing clues about a year before they learn genital differences. There is a long period (roughly three to eight years of age, though strongest around four and five) when the child knows his gender but is not convinced of its permanence. During that time, playing with same-sex peers and rejecting the clothing, toys, and behaviors of the other sex is usually very important. Once gender permanence is realized, boys and girls become less rigid in their stereotyping and their own gender expression.

The gender variant child—who resists or even rejects the gender schema that matches his or her apparent biological sex—has been the subject of increasing research attention in the last decade or so. As with homosexuality in adults, atypical gender identification in children has a history of redefinition and recategorization as scientific evidence and social attitudes have shifted. A boy who insisted that he was a girl, or who preferred feminine clothing and toys, would have once been diagnosed as having gender identity disorder, with a recommended treatment of individual and family therapy to help him conform to cultural expectations. The American Psychological Association is currently revising its *Diagnostic and Statistical Manual of Mental Disorders* for a fifth edition, due in 2013. The proposed version replaces "gender identity disorder"

Important

(GID) with "gender incongruence" and attempts to remove the social stigma associated with the diagnosis. In the meantime, psychiatrists are generally avoiding the GID terminology in favor of "gender dysphoria" or "gender incongruence," and treatment is likely to consist of helping the child and family deal with societal reactions to the child's preferences, such as bullying and teasing. These children and the shifts in their treatment are relevant to the larger study of the history of gendered clothing because they represent a population that is particularly shut out and frustrated by fashions based on a strict boy-girl gender binary.

The cumulative influence of the behavioral science research has been to provide some insight into the mechanism of gender identity acquisition, as it is currently understood. There's the rub: *as currently understood*. Gender theory is expanding, along with the rest of the knowledge universe, and I am fully aware that one of the biggest dangers of interdisciplinary research is that one "leg" of my analysis might be growing at a different rate than the others. In research, as in juggling, the trick is not to achieve perfect timing and balance but to keep the whole system in motion. With this intention, I offer another perspective from which to understand how children's clothing had changed since the late nineteenth century: a generational view of fashion.

FROM GENERATION TO GENERATION: REINVENTING THE FASHION CYCLE

One of the most fundamental endeavors of dress historians has been the attempt to characterize and explain the patterns by which fashions appear, disappear, and then reappear. Whether qualitative (the notion of a "shifting erogenous zone," from legs to breasts to back)[20] or quantitative (Kroeber's careful study of design details and his identification of periodic cycles), all have been based on the paradigm of fashionable clothing as an adult domain. In our texts and classes, we present the history of fashion predominantly as a linear or cyclical progression of women and men who continually adopt new styles and discard old ones. This is generally how I learned fashion history: in 1780, the fashionable woman wore dresses composed of cone-shaped bodices and wide, full skirts. In 1800, she wore diaphanous, column-shaped gowns based on classical antiquity. The difference between 1780 and 1800 was the French Revolution and neoclassicism, which by a complex social, psychological, and cultural process influenced the "fashionable woman." Like most accepted paradigms, its flaws were not evident to me until put to the test in a different environment: children's clothing. This book will offer an alternative view, one based on a generational, developmental paradigm that looks at adults as grown-up children and examines the impact of childhood experiences on adult and children's dress of the next generation.

At first, I worked under the assumption that children's clothing represented a modified version of adult dress, which could be expected to follow the same fashion cycles. Instead, I found that children's clothing represented a highly complex interaction between children and adults, including both parents and grandparents. What children wore could be influenced by their own tastes and preferences (for example, my daughter's assertion in elementary school that leggings were more comfortable than jeans), adult fashion trends (as was often the case in fashionable nineteenth-century children's dress), and their parents' memories of their own childhoods (the red polka dot dress I had to wear in 1956 because my mother wanted one like Shirley Temple's when *she* was little), not to mention grandparents' memories of their children's early years (an article on making a baby's layette advised not to bother making pinning blankets, as elderly relatives would provide them). Sometimes each of these could be seen in distinct styles, but sometimes they blended confusingly together.

Furthermore, what was not obvious to me when I considered the "fashionable woman" became embarrassingly clear when I tried to characterize the "fashionable child." They grow so fast! The fashionable infant of 1900 was the fashionable schoolgirl of 1908 and the fashionable young miss of 1914, and the fashionable woman of 1920 might become the grandmother in a polyester pantsuit in 1973. I found myself following children's fashions not by year or decade but developmentally (by age group) and longitudinally, by generations.

Besides giving me new insights on the mechanisms of children's fashions, this child-centered paradigm suggested something else. If the fashionable infant of 1900 was also the fashionable woman or man of the 1920s, what connections might there be between children's clothing of one era and adult clothing of the next? To what extent is adult clothing a mixture of nostalgia for our favorite childhood garments and images of adults that we observed as children, in addition to our reaction to the truly new styles of our own times? Did the woman of 1800 wear the same styles as the girl of 1780, or is it more accurate to say that the little girls of 1780 grew up to wear the styles of their childhood as young women? Is there a connection between the enormous popularity of jeans and T-shirts for young adults in the late 1960s and early 1970s and their popularity as play clothes for children in the 1950s?

As a further developed example, I investigated a shift I detected in gendered clothing around 1985–86. The mid-1980s witnessed the introduction of "his and hers" disposable diapers, headbands for bald girl babies (serving no function other than as a gender marker), and the disappearance of most unisex baby clothing. Initially, I considered two possible explanations. First, there may have been a correlation with adult fashion trends for the same period. I could see no clear parallel. Although there had been a return to more traditional feminine styles for adults, women still enjoyed considerably more choice dressing themselves than they did when buying clothes for their infants and toddlers. The second possible explanation came from retail buyer friends of mine in department stores, who suggested that manufacturers were individualizing clothing to make it more difficult for people to use hand-me-downs. For those readers inclined to interpret this as a conspiracy against unwilling and powerless parents, the buyer felt that consumers had welcomed the gender-specific styles with surprising enthusiasm. Gender would not have been so successful as an individualizing factor if parents really did not want it. Finally, I realized that I was making the same old assumption about these parents as I once had about the "fashionable woman." They were the same parents, but they had just changed their minds, reversing a gender-neutral trend that started in the early 1970s and then reversing it again within a few years. But were they the same parents? Turning to the United States fertility data, I tracked the number of births by mother and father's birth cohort from 1970 to 1990. A birth cohort is a group of people born in the same years; the Census Bureau uses five-year cohorts and aggregates data every five years, so it is easy to see a given cohort "grow up."

What I found was that the majority of mothers of infants in 1970, 1975, 1980, and 1985 were women born between 1946 and 1960—in other words, they were baby boomers. Men of the same generation were the majority of fathers of infants in 1975, 1980, and 1985. They dominated the birthrate data in 1980, when 79 percent of the mothers and 82 percent of the fathers were between ages twenty and thirty-four.[21] After 1985, their dominance fell off sharply, particularly whatever influence might be due to the first wave of baby boomers, born between 1946 and 1955. Could these demographic changes provide a clue to the gendering of infants' clothing since 1985? Why would the parents' age have an impact on whether babies wore white Pampers or pink Luvs for Her? During the sexual revolution and women's liberation movement of the late 1960s and early 1970s, when appearance was the subject of considerable public and private discourse, the first wave of boomers were teenagers and young adults. The girls and boys of Generation X, who dominated the birthrate data beginning in 1986, were nine or younger when they experienced the same events. What was the difference between the baby boomer experience of the gender bending styles of the 1970s and the experience of Generation X? The child development literature suggests that it is the difference between a child who is still struggling to learn the rules of masculinity and femininity and the older teenager or adult who knows them well enough to modify or resist them. For college students, being taken for a person of the opposite sex (especially by a contemporary of one's parents) might be mildly irritating, or funny, or politically provocative. But for a child—especially one at one of those stages where gender identity is preciously guarded—being mistaken for what you are not can be embarrassing or even threatening. Could that affect how you would dress your own children many years later?

I argue that popularity of unisex infants' styles of the 1970s and early 1980s was partially due to baby boom parents and their rejection of the sexism and highly gendered culture of the 1950s. Younger parents in the mid-1980s had experienced unisex styles and attempts at unisex child rearing as children and viewed them more negatively as adults. This would not be the first time this kind of shift had happened. The "masculinization" of toddler boys' dress took place between 1900 and 1910. That allowed just enough time for the boys of the Little Lord Fauntleroy craze of the late 1880s to grow up and become fathers. (This transition is detailed in chapter 4, "A Boy Is Not a Girl.")

In pursuing this research, I find that I am working in a new and often confusing dimension. It is hard to look at children's clothing and see the connections with the child development literature, which rarely acknowledges changes in fashion. To a historian, it is obvious that the "neutral" styles selected for psychological studies of adult reactions to infants' apparent sex are neutral *only at the time of the study*. Do their findings predict how adults reacted to an infant in a white dress in 1910? Is there a historical difference in reactions to gendered clothing as the "look" of gendered clothing has changed? The nature and impact of childhood experiences are even more difficult to describe without a historical perspective. The APA definitions of gender identity disorder or gender incongruence depend in part on a child's rejection of "expected clothing" for his or her age and sex. Did children experience gender incongruence in the modern clinical sense when toddler clothing was less gender binary and offered more neutral options? It is hard to untangle the threads and see where they lead, but this book is a start, and I hope that it opens a productive collaboration between the humanities, social sciences, and the behavioral sciences on this topic of gender identity formation.

DRESSES ARE
FOR GIRLS AND BOYS

UNDERSTANDING THE PROCESS OF gendering requires not only excavating the process of assigning gender to colors, motifs, and other garment details but focusing on the "white space" between gender markers. The question "What can be worn by either a boy or a girl?" is answered differently throughout this period. For centuries, styles for babies and small children were based on adult women's dress. In the twentieth century, these styles became less and less acceptable, through a process that is as complicated as the clothes themselves are simple.

In order for a child's garment to be gendered, there must be a lexicon of visual cues or patterns of use that are widely understood to be unambiguously masculine or feminine. Without those cues or patterns, the objects are interpreted as neutral, meaning acceptable for both boys and girls. For example, a plain white T-shirt in the 1940s was a masculine garment, based on patterns of use, not its design. At the time, T-shirts were undergarments worn nearly exclusively by men and boys. The same shirt in 2010 is neutral because patterns of use have changed to make T-shirts a staple wardrobe item for women and girls as well. Modifying the shirt with visual cues can assign it a gender—adding cap sleeves and floral appliqué makes it "feminine," for example—but an unadorned white T-shirt is a gender-neutral garment.

For American babies and small children, white dresses were once like T-shirts are today: essentially neutral, though capable of being gendered with the selection of trims and details. Changes in the patterns of use of dresses since the nineteenth century have transformed them from children's clothing to exclusively girls'. Within this transformation, one variation—the white infant dress—had its own peculiar trajectory within the larger story. This chapter begins with an overview of the history of dresses for young children and babies. Part of this story is the recategorization of white dresses from generic and nearly universal wear for children up to the age of five to neutral options for newborns to their current incarnation as a ceremonial style considered acceptable for boys only in the limited context of a traditional christening. The last section of the chapter addresses other dress and skirted styles, once worn by children under five without regard to sex, which faded from use within the span of a generation, beginning around 1900 and disappearing from everyday dress for even the youngest boys by 1920.

DRESSES AND GENDER

Men's and women's clothing in Europe and America was unambiguously gendered for centuries. Why else could cross-dressing be such a successful and persistent motif in folklore and literature? Yes, men's clothing was more ornate and colorful before 1800 than it has been since then. But these elaborate styles had also been undeniably masculine from the late fourteenth century on, when breeches replaced full-length robes for fashionable men. Only men wore trousers in any form (even underdrawers were verboten for women), and what is a codpiece if not a sign of gender? Clothing for infants, in contrast, made no distinction between boys and girls and was patterned on women's clothing in decoration and some aspects of design, such as neckline and bodice constructions. The elements we see as "feminine"—skirts, elaborate trimming, and long hair—represented a more complicated conflation of effeminacy, dependency, and sexual detachment associated with women and with infants of both sexes. To fully understand this requires learning to see nineteenth-century fashions through contemporary eyes.

Long before clothing for the youngest children acquired gender symbolism, by far the most significant message it conveyed was age. Before the eighteenth century, there were only three broad categories of clothing, which signified a mixture of age, gender, and occupation: infant clothes (diapers, swaddling, and long dresses), trousered styles (most men and boys over the age of about seven years), and skirted styles (women, male clergy, and children under seven). Within these categories there were many nuanced variations; for example, although most men wore some kind of bifurcated lower garments, sailors, peasants, and laborers wore loose trousers, while fitted breeches were a mark of gentility. Children's clothing as we know it did not exist, nor did "teen" fashion.

Before gender symbolism could be added to children's clothing, the notion of "children's clothing" itself had to be invented and refined. We use the terms "toddler" and "preschoolers" to signify various subdivisions of children under the age of five, but the exact meaning of those words, like the clothing associated with them, is a recent innovation.[1]

When people in the eighteenth century spoke of an infant, they meant a child who could not yet walk. The demarcation line between infancy and childhood was when the baby stood upright and could walk. This was such an important milestone that it was signaled with a change of wardrobe from the long, loose gowns of infancy to small versions of adult clothing. Infants and young children wore skirts, and young children's styles were virtually identical to those of adult women. Not until around the age of seven were boys "breeched," or put into their first pair of trousers. It was much more important to observe age conventions than it is for us today: dressing a three-year-old boy in a man's suit would have been unthinkable. According to material culture scholar Karin Calvert, childhood frocks served the purpose of visually connecting the babies and small children to the world of women.[2] This explanation seems reasonable, especially in the larger context of the scientific logic of the time that posited great differences between men's and women's brains and perceived women as an incomplete or immature form of men.[3]

The popular divisions of childhood stages shifted in the late nineteenth century, and with that shift came the first gender distinctions. By that time, the word "toddler" was gaining currency, used to denote children about one or two years old, still babyish in form and uncertain of gait.[4] The age of breeching for boys fell to around four or five years, although the transition was not to full-length trousers but to short pants or knickerbockers, which maintained the convention of age-defined clothing. This had the dual effect of reducing the age range for which neutral clothing was appropriate and gendering the clothing of four-year-olds, even though girls' fashions did not really change. Dressing little boys like big boys helped define skirts (and eventually other design details) once worn by all toddlers as feminine by default.

CHILDREN'S DRESSES

This saga of gendered clothing begins in the 1880s, but a bit of background is necessary to place it in context. Children's clothing had already been invented and redefined several times in the previous two hundred years. The concepts of "infant" and "child" have never been static. Historians of childhood date the emergence of the concept of an ensouled infant or an autonomous child in Europe to the mid-eighteenth century, and dress historians note that until that same period there was really no such thing as children's clothing.[5] Beliefs about children had shifted significantly in the early nineteenth century. The concept of a child's mind and character as a blank slate was giving way to a romantic, sentimental view of children as innately good creatures, closer to perfection than adults. The boundary between infancy and childhood was clearly marked in dress: babies wore simple, unfitted dresses, usually white, and children wore essentially the same clothing as adults, with the exception of little boys, who wore skirts until they were old enough to be "breeched," at about six or seven. The transition from infancy to childhood (from white dresses to more colorful children's dresses) took place sometime between the ages of one and two, when the youngster was walking steadily and no longer needed diapers.[6]

The year 1900 would mark not only the end of a century but also the approach of the close of an entire millennium. While the psychological impact of the phrase "the twentieth century" is lost to us, who are so familiar with it, to the generation who witnessed the passing of one century to another, it seemed a dramatic marker. The first millennium had witnessed nearly all of the rise and fall of the Roman Empire. During the second millennium, Western Europe had emerged as the heir to Rome's legacy. In the view of many Americans, the third millennium would belong to them and their descendants. Westward expansion nourished dreams of an empire to rival those of Rome and Great Britain. With popular interest in the future increased almost to the point of being an obsession, American children could hardly remain untouched. The last generation born in the nineteenth century was regarded not merely as tomorrow's adults but as the first generation of a vastly different new age. Not since the American Revolution had so much hope been invested in this country's children.

But, as many pessimistic writers of the period noted, American children of the 1890s seemed distressingly different from their counterparts of the Revolutionary and early Federal periods. Life was easier, childhood was longer and more sheltered, and the children were softer and more pampered—or so it seemed to those who saw in American youth not its triumph but its downfall. The evolutionary theories of naturalist Charles Darwin had been adapted into a popular belief now called "social Darwinism," which held that the human struggle for survival and supremacy required dramatic transformations from generation to generation. The agents of change were not only the environment and sexual selection but also parents and educators, who had the power to mold the coming generation into the required shape. If the twentieth century was to belong to America, the children who would inherit that empire must be made fit to rule it.

Children born at the turn of the century were not only the focus of a good portion of millennial fervor but also the objects of unprecedented scientific scrutiny. In the 1880s, G. Stanley Hall published the first of many scholarly and popular works on child psychology, the field he pioneered with his studies of intelligence in children. By 1896, the influence of psychological studies was so widespread that a July 1896 *Delineator* article, "The Baby's Outfit," could base its recommendations for nursery decorations on studies of infant development. Pediatric medicine was emerging as a specialization, providing new information on the physical development of children. Graduate degrees and university research in education created a new category of experts, educational theorists, who influenced teachers and parents alike. Finally, the emergence of the home economics profession provided an emphasis on the scientific approach to every aspect of domestic life, including food, clothing, shelter, and childcare. College-educated home economists promoted a new, rational model of modern homemaking through their public roles as teachers, rural extension agents, and journalists.

Considering the character traits that the leaders of the twentieth century would need, Stanford University president David Jordan predicted that the coming times would be "strenuous, complex, and democratic."[7] These characteristics would challenge all American youth, of all classes and backgrounds, to be physically tough and mentally alert. William Russ Ward struck a similar chord in his 1896 *Outlook* article, "Our Boys," which listed planning, alertness, capacity for work, and fitness as requisites for success. The idea of physical fitness was especially important to contemporary writers, who felt that athletic training would provide the physical health that "soft" American boys and girls were lacking and encourage the development of desirable mental and social skills. Theodore Roosevelt wrote many articles endorsing sports and physical fitness, including one in *St. Nicholas,* a children's magazine, where he encouraged young boys to get involved in rough sports.[8] According to Roosevelt, physically demanding sports taught endurance and courage and channeled children's physical energy toward a goal. Competitive sports—playing to win—were better than just running around.

Living in a post-Freudian world, it may be hard to believe there was a time when infancy was not seen through the lens of popular psychology, with its baggage of sexual development through attachment to the mother. Pre-Freudian baby boys were not perceived as masculine, and to say otherwise was in very poor taste. "Masculine" connoted "manly," in the adult sense, and only grown men were manly. Manliness had a whiff of sexuality to it as well, so to describe a toddler as "manly" had a risqué air to it, like referring to a little girl as a "hottie" would be today. Schoolboys were a bit masculine, and adolescent boys more so, since sexual, intellectual, and emotional maturity was thought to be acquired gradually. Boys' clothing reflected the prevailing beliefs, summarized by historian Joseph Kett, that maturation took place in distinct stages and that "precocity," or early attainment of maturity, was dangerous to the developing child.[9] The blossoming of the field of child psychology and of the children's clothing industry worked in tandem to invent the symbolic "baby" and "child."[10] If there was a silver lining to the influence of psychoanalysis on parenting, it was the recognition of the child in every adult, inspiring new empathy for children's dreams and fears. The downside of this was the ensuing trend toward what sociologist Daniel Cook labels "pediocularity," or shifting the child's point of view to the center, to the point of usurping the adult perspective.[11]

To say that infants' clothing became more gendered between 1890 and 1910 is misleading in its passivity and in its implied equivalence. Infants' clothing did not become more gendered; parents began to dress their children in more gendered ways. And they did not dress girls in "girlier" ways and boys more like little men; they invested much more effort in masculinizing their sons than feminizing their daughters, because fear of sexual depravity—particularly the supposed physical and psychological danger of masturbation and the threat of homosexuality—was focused almost completely on boys.

If it puzzles twenty-first-century readers to learn that Victorian parents preferred their babies to look like asexual cherubs, their amusement with the ensuing gender confusion will probably come as an even greater

MELLIN'S FOOD BABIES
Result of the Guessing Contest

The above portraits were shown in our exhibit at the St. Louis Exposition. We offered $250.00 in gold to the person who could correctly guess the boys and girls in the 20 numbered pictures.

No one guessed 20 correctly.

Mr. George Harrison, Enfield, N. C., was awarded the $250.00, the only person guessing 18 correctly, this being the largest number of correct guesses.

Mellin's Food received the GRAND PRIZE, higher than the Gold Medal, the Highest Award of the St. Louis Exposition 1904.

No other infants' food received so high an award.

MELLIN'S FOOD CO.,   BOSTON, MASS.

Mellin's Food advertisement, showing the results of a sex-guessing contest in *Ladies' Home Journal* in 1905. No one guessed all twenty correctly.

Courtesy of the Warshaw Collection of Business Americana–Periodicals, Archives Center, National Museum of American History, Behring Center, Smithsonian Institution.

shock. Adults in the days of neutral baby clothing were well aware that, without clothing clues, sex was impossible to discern in infants. Newborn babies don't look like boys and girls at all; they more closely resemble wrinkled and toothless old men. The makers of Mellin's baby food recognized the humor value of this in their 1905 sex-guessing contest. Mellin's ad featuring twenty babies in the *Ladies' Home Journal* promised a generous reward to readers who accurately guessed the sex of the most babies. When the contest results were revealed in a later issue, not one contestant had correctly guessed the sex of all twenty babies. It is very hard to imagine twenty-first-century parents submitting their child's photo to a nationwide magazine in the hope of "stumping" readers on their baby's sex.

A *New York Times* reporter covering a "baby show" at the Westchester, New York, County Fair joked in his article, "It Was Babies' Day," that "the gentleman babies occupied one side of the house while their sisters were made the attraction on the other. Only the judges knew which was which. There was nothing to inform the novice in babydom to which quarter he must look to see the prototype of himself." These examples show us just how different we are from our ancestors on the subject of infants' gender. Whereas modern parents work to eliminate gender ambiguity, their great-grandparents found it natural and amusing.

It's not unusual to hear modern people describe Victorian babies as being dressed like girls; this is an error. To its own parents and grandparents, a child wearing the traditional white dress looked like "a baby." This convention could be explained in practical terms of diapering, hand-me-downs, and laundering, but that is a partial truth. An equally important explanation is that gendered dress was considered inappropriate for young children, whose asexual innocence was so often cited as one of their greatest charms. The feminine aspects of their clothing probably have as much to do with idealized aspects of femininity—dependence, chastity, and delicacy—that were also associated with infancy.

The popular meanings of the words "masculine" or "manly" and "feminine" or "womanly" have not changed markedly since the mid-nineteenth century, particularly in their sexual overtones. We may be more careful not to ascribe personality traits such as "ambitious" or "nurturing" to men and women as a class, but the old roles of pursuer/pursued, aggressive/passive, and the sexual double standard are still bundled with biological sex in popular culture. The main difference is that few parents in 1880 would be comfortable dressing their year-old son to express his masculinity or choosing clothing to accentuate their infant daughter's femininity, and modern American parents are equally uncomfortable with gender ambiguity. Between 1890 and the end of World War II, infancy and early childhood had been transformed from a gender-free zone populated by white-clad cherubs to an era of emerging gender signifiers such as pink and blue. What happened to make gender coding acceptable, instead of anathema?

Between 1890 and 1920, bifurcation, a garment feature considered masculine just a generation earlier, became redefined as "neutral," at least situationally. We'll explore this more closely in the next chapter. Dresses for children ages four through seven were reclassified as "feminine," and a very subtle struggle to negotiate the gender of other details began. These details included hat styles, floral and animal motifs, overlap of the front opening, and, most visibly, the gender connotations of pink and blue. By the end of this period, around 1920, the rules for neutral styles for infants and toddlers had recrystallized in patterns that would not change again until the 1960s. Newborn infants of both sexes continued to wear dresses, though rompers and other one-piece garments gradually replaced them except for special occasions. Toddler boys and girls could wear identical play clothes, coats, and snowsuits, but dressy occasions called for more gendered styles. Boys' clothing continued to feature fabrics and decorations that would be considered feminine today.

THE WHITE DRESS FROM UNIFORM TO FOSSILIZED FASHION

Compared with fashionable dress for women and children, or even men, clothing for babies was practically a uniform for generations. Everyday dress for European and American infants up through the late nineteenth century varied according to class and climate, from nakedness or a diaper and a long shirt to several layers of clothing, but that clothing was always skirted. Male and female infants alike wore dresses that ended a foot or more beyond their toes; the long skirt helped keep the baby's feet and legs warm. Once a child began to walk upright, shorter skirts and dresses replaced the long gowns. Baby clothing resisted change in general—and the imposition of gender in particular—longer than styles for toddlers and preschoolers.

The christening gown was probably the most iconic garment in a nineteenth-century infant's wardrobe, although most children never had one. The christening gown was simply a more ornate version of everyday

Baby in christening dress, 1899–1900.
Daniel Murray Collection, Library of Congress.

clothing, worn for a special occasion, in the same way that wedding gowns of the period were identical in length and design to women's dresses of the era. Using a unique garment only for a single occasion—whether a baptism or a wedding—was out of reach for most Americans before the twentieth century. Still, christening gowns provide an important starting point for any consideration of baby clothing, because of their relationship to everyday dress and what they reveal about infancy.

Centuries before christening gowns became popular for baptismal use, parents used the chrisom cloth, a piece of white linen saturated with holy oil that was placed over the child's face during the ritual. By the Elizabethan period, the chrisom cloth had grown large enough to wrap the child entirely and was also used as a shroud if the baby died within weeks of birth. (The term "chrisom" referred to the baby itself, eventually coming to mean a child who died within a month after birth or before being baptized.) The choice of pure white linen was not accidental—white had symbolized purity long before the dawn of the Christian era. In very wealthy families, a bearing cloth, an elaborate outer covering in white or occasionally red (the color of the Holy Spirit), could accompany the chrisom cloth. By the mid-nineteenth century the christening gown (or robe) had replaced the chrisom cloth and acquired the elaborate decoration of the bearing cloth. Symbolically, the christening gown represented both the innocence of the child and the economic status of its family. Gender symbolism was conspicuous by its absence.

To the uninitiated, all baby dresses from the nineteenth century look like christening gowns. The fact that these dresses exist by the dozens in large costume collections, and that babies were rarely painted or photographed in anything other than a long, white elaborate dress, indicates that these were part of an everyday wardrobe. While every detail—the length, the intricate decoration, and the pristine white fabric—translates into "special occasion" to the modern eye, long white dresses were standard issue clothing for middle- and upper-class babies in America and Europe for centuries.

Besides symbolizing purity and innocence, white had practical advantages. As a mothers' advice columnist in *Peterson's Magazine* pointed out, white clothes showed dirt better, so it would be changed more frequently, and some colors were produced using potentially harmful dyes and mordants. In addition, many writers pointed out that white linen or cotton could be boiled or bleached without fading and stood up better to vigorous scrubbing.

Baby paper dolls before 1910 were sometimes identified by sex, but usually not, just as "the baby" in literature and correspondence nearly always occupied a gender-free world. Unlike modern advice books and columns, mothers' manuals in the nineteenth century comfortably used "it" to refer to babies after as well as before their arrival. In those rare cases when paper doll infants are identified as boys, their appearance gives no evidence of any subtle gender markers; all wear white dresses, some plain, some fancy, but identical to those worn by baby girls. Babies were also popular on advertising and greeting cards (particularly representing Baby New Year). Sometimes the child's sex is suggested through props; a trade

Sister and baby brother, ca. 1905. Both wear
traditional white baby dresses, in lengths appropriate
to their ages.

University of Maryland Costume and Textile Collection.

card for a hat manufacturer displays a tot in a knee-length white dress,
pink sash, and blue socks, trying on a man's top hat.[12] But more often
the sex of the child was left to the imagination of the child playing with
the paper doll. Uncut examples of the 1894 McLaughlin XXXX Coffee
toddler paper doll exist, clad in a white dress and light blue sacque-type
jacket, identified only as "baby." The example in the Winterthur Museum

and Library has been cut out and named "Robert," the name scrawled in a childish hand on the back.[13]

THE FEMINIZING OF DRESSES FOR CHILDREN

For most of the eighteenth and nineteenth centuries, there was little distinction made between the clothing for a two-year old and for a six-year old. This age range was divided in the early twentieth century into toddlers (one- and two-year-olds) and preschoolers, and it was at that point that gender distinctions were also introduced. Prior to 1900, variations according to gender appear in some portraits and descriptions of individual children, but most dress historians believe that these did not constitute uniform rules. In an era where sartorial boundaries between men and women or between children and adults were clear and unambiguous, variations that are subtle and inconsistent seem unlikely to be intended as "rules."

One possible variation was the use of "leading strings" (fabric strips attached to the shoulders of garments, used like reins to control small children); some portraits appear to depict girls wearing leading strings at an older age than boys. Another difference was in the shape of the upper part of older children's dresses: middle- and upper-class boys and girls both wore long-skirted dresses, but the bodices on boys' dresses were sometimes shaped more like a man's doublet than a woman's bodice.[14] In the second half of the nineteenth century, skirted styles for boys under the age of six were more likely to be pleated into the waistband, while girls' skirts were more likely to be gathered. Little girls' skirts sometimes featured horizontal tucks, which could be released to make the dress longer. Boys' skirts usually lacked these growth features, because they would exchange dresses for trousers around the time of the toddler-to-child growth spurt. But none of these rules or patterns was applied consistently, as would be expected if clear gender distinctions had been their purpose. Modern curators and historians are more likely to label the young subject of a painting or photograph an "unidentified child" than to take a chance on guessing wrong.

This lack of unambiguous, consistent gender coding leads us to the conclusion that most young children's clothing in the nineteenth century was perceived as neutral, in the sense of being appropriate for either boys or girls and giving no clue to the child's sex. The design may look "feminine" to us today, and it is hard to tell if it also had that connotation at the time. At the very least, the notion of male infants having more in common with women than men was not a source of discomfort at the time, or the conventions would have been different, regardless of practical considerations. In contrast, age distinctions had been increasingly important since the late eighteenth century, when styles distinctly for children had been introduced, bridging the years between infancy and adulthood. In the nineteenth century, children's fashions were further subdivided into two groups: styles for school-age children and a new category for children under six or seven years. These new styles appeared gradually over the first half of the century and were commonplace by the 1850s. From 1820 through the 1840s, fashions for little children were very much miniature versions of women's clothing, with the main distinctions found in the fit of the bodice and the length of the skirt. In fashionable clothing for women, the bodice gradually lengthened and became more tapered, extending to a deep V-shape by the late 1840s. At the same time, the waistline for young children conformed to the natural waistline or fell just slightly above it, displaying their more pear-shaped torsos. Light stays were used for little girls to help shape their figures, and there is some evidence that boys' dresses sometimes featured boning or were worn with corsets. A slightly looser fit allowed for both movement and growth. In the 1820s, children's dresses became much shorter than women's, usually reaching to a point between the calf and the knee. This revealed the white cotton drawers, or pantalettes, which had been worn by children since around 1800. These undergarments became longer and more elaborate, filling the gap between hem and boot top; some illustrations show their decorative edges extending a good six to eight inches below the skirt. Both boys and girls wore pantalettes: a short story in *Godey's* refers to a well-educated young man having started school when he was still "a little fellow in his pantalettes."[15] These were essentially two separate legs gathered into a flat waistband but with an open crotch from front to back. "Closed drawers," with a completely sewn crotch seam, were not commonly used until the 1870s or 1880s.

The fabrics chosen for little children's clothing were somewhat different from those used for older children and women. In the first place, many of the prints and patterns popular for women's fashions were too large to be used for children. Modish styles for women could be adapted for children by using small-scale designs if they were available; plaids, checks, and tiny calico prints were often used. But very often the best choice was a solid-color fabric. Similarly, trims had to be scaled down, and *Godey's* recommended omitting the trim altogether rather than applying machine-made trimming that was too large for the child's body. In the 1840s, there was some indication that manufacturers were beginning to produce fabrics scaled specifically for children: tiny floral prints went out of style for women, but remained on the market as a perennial favorite for children's clothing.

It is very hard to distinguish between boys and girls in illustrations or portraits dating before 1850. The cut of their clothing was virtually identical, and lace, ribbon, and braided trim were used for both boys and girls. Girls' dresses were made up in floral fabric more often than were boys' styles, and both *Godey's* and *Peterson's* recommended dark neutral colors (brown, black, gray) more often for boys. But outside of these few not-very-firm rules, most dresses for little children give no clue to the sex of the wearer. Accessories help a little. Girls' hair is sometimes longer, even long enough to be styled in a simple version of women's hairstyles, with long love locks on either side of the face. But most little children in portraits or fashion plates have hair that is about chin-length and very simply parted and combed. Sandals were more often worn by girls and boots by boys, though that is not a consistent pattern. Sometimes the artist may give additional clues to the child's identity: a drum or a toy whip for a little boy, a doll for a girl. But a modern curator in a museum, faced with an unaccessorized dress and not a scrap of information, must describe the garment just as *Godey's* would have—a child's dress.

Skirt length was key to age-appropriate children's dresses. Advice writers recommended a gradual descent, with slightly lower hems each year. (This seems so labor-intensive that it begs the question of how carefully the advice was followed.) The gap between ankle and hem was filled using pantalettes through the 1860s and the long stockings for the rest of the century. Juanita Jenson's recent research on photographs of children suggests another possible clue: girls' dresses have horizontal tucks in the skirt to allow for lengthening them, and boys' dresses generally do not, since as they grew taller they would transition to trousers.[16] Throughout infancy and early childhood, boys and girls led very similar lives in the nineteenth century. But by the time they reached the age of five or six, their paths were beginning to diverge. Boys were more likely to be educated at school than at home, and they were starting to engage more in

masculine activities, whether man's work or boy's play. By the same token, boys' and girls' clothing styles lost much of their similarity, though
this is more evident in boys' dress than in girls'. One writer for *Harper's
Magazine* explained it in symbolic terms in December 1876: "The girl
wears forever the infant petticoat, with all its power and privileges."

In the second half of the century, women's magazines featured fashions for toddlers and children under seven much more often than styles
for infants or for older children. This was largely because infants' costume changed so slowly and older children's clothing was usually a shorter, simpler version of adult dress. In contrast, fashions for small children
combined trends in women's clothing with a strong element of fantasy
that resulted in styles that were distinctly childlike and picturesque.

The 1870s and 1880s marked the high point of elaborate dress for
children (or the low point, according to its critics). Closely reflecting
trends in women's fashions, a single outfit might be made up in two or
three fabrics and trimmed in as many different trims. Every possible historical, literary, and fantastic source was exploited for design inspiration,
particularly for little boys, who appeared in the guise of sailors, cavaliers,
highlanders, and numerous others. Kilts, with their masculine connotation and endorsement by Queen Victoria for her own sons, were particularly popular for little boys too young for trousers but ready to put
aside baby dresses. These picturesque styles signaled a new willingness to
distinguish boys from girls while at the same time avoiding obvious adult
masculine styling, thereby preserving the important age distinction.

THE DECLINE AND DISAPPEARANCE
OF WHITE BABY DRESSES

The white infant dress fell out of favor as a wardrobe staple very
gradually. The very long dresses of the nineteenth century were replaced
by first dresses that were still below the baby's toes by several inches, worn
for the first few months. The transition from the first dresses to "short
clothes" was a sufficiently significant milestone to be listed in baby record
books along with "first tooth" and "first steps" until the 1930s. Advice
columnists suggested that short clothes should be adopted when the baby
began to creep, but the completed baby books at UCLA tell a different
story. Between 1900 and 1915, most record the adoption of short dresses
at six months or less, with about a third between two and four months,

Boy, age four or five, in a dress with pleated skirt (ca. 1870).
University of Maryland Costume and Textile Collection.

and the average age continued to drop through the 1920s. By the 1930s, short clothes are rarely noted, or the page is marked with a perfunctory comment "at birth" or "from the beginning." The white baby dress did not completely disappear from boys' wardrobes; it was still favored for newborns in the late 1940s. Sears, Roebuck & Co. included dresses in its basic packaged layettes until 1945 and in deluxe layettes until 1959.

One explanation for the patterns we see in gendered and neutral children's clothing is the way in which clothing was made and acquired.

Most infants' and children's clothes were made at home. Baby layette items, in particular, were seen as the special responsibility of the expectant mother and her close female relatives, with a great premium placed on "fine sewing" skills. While magazine descriptions of clothes for girls' and little children's clothing typically included expressions of delight and enjoyment of the task of making or selecting their clothes, columns on boys' clothing were much less enthusiastic. Once it lost its resemblance to women's clothing in fabric and construction, boys' clothing became more of a problem for mothers to make at home. Women's magazines did carry regular illustrations and descriptions of clothing for older boys, but often indicated that the actual creation of such garments as suits and coats would be delegated to the same tailor who made clothes for the boy's father. Ready-to-wear clothing was available for boys in this age group earlier than for other children, well before the Civil War. Shirts and everyday knickerbockers were still within the skills of the average home seamstress. It is possible—even likely—that the trend toward a lower age of breeching boys parallels the expansion of mass-produced boys' wear into smaller sizes. What is less clear at this point is which came first.

Traditional white dresses for little boys and girls, once chosen because they could be bleached to their original whiteness, were replaced by darker colors that showed the dirt less. This reform was for the mother's sake as well as the children's, part of an effort to rearrange her workload so that she could spend more time with her children and less with their laundry. The modern mother made (or bought) clothing that was simple and easy to maintain rather than spending hours sewing on ruffles or bleaching and starching white dresses. Ready-to-wear clothing was an increasingly popular alternative to homemade clothing, especially for boys' suits and play clothes for both girls and boys.

Most of the advice offered about clothing in books and magazines dealt with practical and moral questions, not stylistic ones. Authors were understandably vague about the correct choice of color, fabric, and design for children's clothing, since fashions could be expected to change rapidly. But most did include discussions of the principles that should guide mothers in dressing their children. Simplicity was stressed most often, even as the plain, easy-fitting styles of the early Federal period went out of style in the first half of the century and were replaced by the excesses of midcentury fashion. Advice and practice do not necessarily coincide in matters of both childcare and dress. In 1831, *Godey's Magazine and*

Lady's Book noted in "Woman at Home" that a mother's character and care are reflected in her children's appearance, which should unite "simplicity with taste." Many other writers also pointed out the connection between simplicity of dress and developing a strong moral sense in children. Excessive finery encouraged vanity and extravagance. By the same token, children should not be rewarded with new clothing. Dress was to be treated as secondary, with little attention paid to distinctions in color, fabric, or style. In reality, this advice was widely ignored; children's clothing followed the growing elaboration of women's clothing throughout the century. By the late 1860s, writers contrasted contemporary children's heavily trimmed costumes of silk and fine wool with their grandparents' plain washable frocks and skeleton suits and lamented the demise of simplicity in children's dress. The style was not to change until the end of the century. In the meantime, fashion would continue to make the child look like "an artificial, spoiled or excessively grave household pet or live doll."[17]

Although children's health had always been an important concern for parents, particularly when infant and child mortality was high, the relationship between clothing and good health was not clearly understood. Mothers' manuals offered a variety of suggestions, some of them in conflict with others. Should clothing cover the body evenly, or should some parts of the body (feet, trunk) be covered with extra layers for warmth? Should underwear be made of cotton or wool? Would going barefoot and hatless help prevent disease by "hardening" a child or make him more vulnerable to illness? Then, as now, mothers did their best, relying on their own instincts and experiences as well as the advice of relatives and published "experts."

When children's clothing finally began to lose its fantastic look in the 1880s, the change was advocated on practical rather than moral grounds. Simple, washable clothing was more hygienic. The emerging conviction that vigorous activity was good for children also did away with clothing styles that were too fragile, restrictive, or hard to clean. The way to keep children clean was with regular baths, not with inactivity.

What is left out of the advice literature is discussion of the role that clothing might play in learning appropriate gender roles or identity. There is the explicit expectation that girls would eventually follow their mothers' lead in developing taste and expertise in clothing, first for their dolls and themselves and eventually for their households. Boys' task of learning about clothing and grooming was mentioned much less. It appears to be assumed that they would learn enough about clothing to dress presentably according to their class (ordering suits from a tailor, tying a cravat), with the lessons left to the father and therefore missing from mothers' manuals. In both cases, gender lessons were deferred until middle childhood, when they entered school. Baby dolls were listed in the UCLA baby books as common first-birthday gifts for boys as well as girls.

THE PRIVATE AND PUBLIC LIVES OF SMALL CHILDREN

Parallel to the creation of a "separate sphere" for genteel women was the construction of the ideal childhood as one in which the cares and dangers of adulthood were never allowed to intrude, a second sphere nestled within the realm of women, first at home and later at school. For very little children, advice authors disagreed over the best age for beginning formal schooling. The suggested age ranged from six to eight. Mothers were to ensure that their children already knew their letters and numbers (and their manners) before they entered school. There were exceptions to the age rules, as in the case of Harriet Robinson's youngest brother, who attended Lowell's free school at age three.[18]

Children's lives gradually became more public, and eventually babies joined their older siblings in emerging from the nursery. In the first half of the nineteenth century, the youngest babies in middle- and upper-class homes rarely left the nursery, and babies under one year rarely left the house. In "The Nursery" in March 1852, *Godey's* describes a dress for a baby "old enough to be called for to show to company." The introduction of the first baby carriage in 1848, designed by a New Yorker, eventually made babies more involved in their parents' social activities. Infants' fashions found in magazines from the second half of the century are more elaborate and include many styles for "visiting" or "walking."

The "hand-me down" explanation for baby dresses seems plausible on its face, but is not entirely satisfactory, especially for the first half of the century, before fabrics and trims became plentiful. *Godey's* suggested that baby's dresses and underslips be one yard long for daily wear and a yard and a half or two yards long for more public events such as "visiting and christening."[19] When the baby was beginning to crawl, between four and eight months of age, a mother could expect to spend considerable time shortening all of his skirts, slips, and dresses to just about floor length. In this way, the newborn's layette could be worn throughout most of the

Baby, nine–twelve months, in short white
dress, early 1900s.

Photograph by W. A. Pixley, Library of Congress.

first year and practically be worn out in the process. With the advent
of abundant elaborate trimmings, long dresses began to feature several
inches of trimming at the hem, so shortening a dress would require more
than just raising the hem; at that point, long dresses were more likely to
be saved for a later baby, and new short dresses were made or acquired for
the toddler. This might explain the closets full of long dresses from the
late nineteenth century in costume collections across the country. The
other explanation is that long dresses were falling out of favor; *Peterson's*

advised in 1885 that "dresses should be short; keep feet and legs warm with stockings, not the dress."[20] Between 1880 and 1920, baby dresses sold through Sears, Roebuck catalogs became progressively shorter.

1902–1917	27"
1917–1919	choice of 24" ("semi-long") or 27"
1920–1927	24"
1928–1931	choice of 20" ("short") or 24" ("long")
1932–1959	20"

Given that the average length of a newborn infant is 20 inches, even the shortest "short" dress would fall several inches beyond the baby's toes. Evidence from the UCLA baby books further clarifies actual practice. Until the 1910s, ankle-length clothes were generally introduced at around five to six months, but by 1925 the transition was rarely recorded.

During the same twenty-year period, skirted styles for toddler boys also disappeared. Some authorities laid out strict rules for dressing, according to age. *Vogue* in 1900 outlined the stages of boy-dressing very specifically: long dresses until six months, then short dresses until age three, then either Russian blouses with knickers or kilt suits up to the age of five or six.[21] *Harper's Bazaar* noted that boys were usually put into trousers "as soon as they were too old for baby frocks," at about three years.[22] Despite this advice, toddler boys photographed between 1890 and 1910 and boy paper dolls were increasingly less likely to be wearing skirts and more likely to be wearing knickers. Some toddler-sized kilt suits even came with matching knickers, giving parents the choice to put their son in a kilt, trousers, or both, depending on the occasion. By the 1920s, dresses were consistently limited to infants and girls, with toddler boys nearly always wearing some form of trousers.

Short dresses, while still worn by very young babies, began to appear in "girl" and "boy" styles in the twentieth century. An advertisement in the 1939 *Vogue Patterns* for boys' dresses shows two styles (sized six and twelve months), both featuring belts and double-breasted styles. When I asked my mother-in-law if my husband (b. 1949) had ever worn baby dresses, she responded, "Of course not. He just wore robes," and showed me his christening gown as an example: a long, white cotton garment styled exactly like a bathrobe, opening completely in the front and featuring a corded belt. From her description, he also wore less elaborate "robes" that were more like loose kimonos. Not all boys would have worn such items; my brother (b. 1947) wore short white cotton batiste dresses for his first month, similar to the styles shown in Sears, Roebuck catalogs throughout the 1940s and 1950s. This does suggest that by the 1940s, even short dresses for boys were falling from popular use. By the 1960s, dresses for boys were limited to christening styles, and the transformation of dresses from age-appropriate neutral clothing for children under seven into gender-appropriate clothing for girls and women was complete.

It is important to point out, first of all, that these changes in the popular usage of children's dresses occurred outside of the cycles of adult fashion in the late nineteenth and early twentieth centuries. Whatever relationship may have existed between baby-dressing and women's clothing trends was superficial: fabrication, trim, and other details. These details connected baby clothing to women's fashions but did not generally distinguish between boys and girls, except toward the end of dresses' reign as neutral garments. Practical considerations such as diapering and the economy of hand-me-downs may have been a factor, but those considerations still exist, and boys no longer wear dresses. Dresses would be more comfortable than pants in hot weather, but men do not wear them for the same reason that boys don't: because they are feminine garments. This transformation happened so recently that there are men living today who wore dresses as children, and it took place so thoroughly that we appear to have forgotten that dresses were ever for boys as well as girls.

PANTS ARE FOR BOYS AND GIRLS

THE IMPORTANCE OF WEARING PANTS

From the end of the fourteenth century on, the most obvious difference between men's and women's clothing in Europe was that men's legs were visible—encased in stockings, breeches, or trousers—and women's were covered by skirts. European images of Muslim and Chinese women were made more exotic by their wearing trousers. (Thus the old expression "wearing the pants in the family," referring to family authority.) When, in the 1850s, early feminists Elizabeth Cady Stanton and Amelia Bloomer adopted full Turkish-inspired trousers worn under calf-length dresses, it ignited a culture war. The history of the gender significance of trousers, breeches, and other bifurcated forms of dress is complicated and would take us too far astray, so here is the condensed version.

Long ago, whether one wore a skirt or trousers was a matter of culture or class, not sex. In her groundbreaking 1973 exhibit catalog, *Cut My Cote,* Dorothy Burnham demonstrated that the choice of shaped (trousers) or draped (skirts) garments was initially technological, stemming from the desire to create body coverings from the most available materials with a minimum of waste. For societies whose most abundant materials were animal hides, the shape of those skins lent themselves to garments with fitted arms and legs. Agricultural societies developed fibers such as wool, silk, and linen along with the technologies (spinning, weaving) for turning them into cloth, resulting in garments based on rectangles. These basic forms were eventually retained even as the available materials expanded to include both skins and cloth. In 1000 CE, both women and men in Persia and Mongolia wore trousers and coats or jackets with fitted sleeves, and both men and women in Constantinople wore long robes.

This pattern was complicated as conquest and trade resulted in the mingling of styles and materials, and the choice of trousers or skirts

acquired a new connotation: power and status. Trouser-wearing hunt-
ers of northern Europe adopted the draped, loosely fitted forms of the
Roman Empire as symbols of power and citizenship. Between the fifth
and early fourteenth centuries, upper-class men, women, and children in
Europe wore long robes or skirts that were very similar in cut, with fitted
stockings underneath for warmth. Farmers and tradesmen wore shorter
robes, more like long shirts, along with visible trousers. Women of the
same class wore their skirts shorter than those of gentlewomen. Visible
trousers, then, were associated with lower-class men, not with masculinity in general. Long skirts, being worn by upper-class men and women,
were a mark of gentility.

During the fourteenth century, the robes of fashionable men became
dramatically shorter, reaching just below the buttocks and even higher.
Their stockings grew longer, until the two legs were joined at the waist
and a piece of fabric, or codpiece, was added to cover the genitals. The
resulting garments eventually divided into upper and lower hose, and the
upper hose became breeches. By the fifteenth century, skirts or gowns
were worn by women of all classes, breeches were for upper-class men,
and trousers were worn by the working class. At the end of the eighteenth
century, breeches fell from favor and full-length trousers became the accepted lower garment for nearly all men.

It is important to point out that European men's and women's clothing had been moving apart for centuries. By the last quarter of the nineteenth century, it was clear at a glance that men and women were different creatures, with different characteristics, abilities, and destinies. After
generations of expressive sensuality, men's clothing became increasingly
plain, drab, and practical, in contrast to women's much more elaborate
and restrictive dress. The challenge for parents was to fit male children
into this pattern—when and how to differentiate them from their sisters and when and how to connect them to their fathers. This was not
a simple matter, at a time when appropriate dress was determined by a
complicated mix of gender, age, activity, and socioeconomic status.

BOYS AND BREECHING

Before the middle of the eighteenth century, there really was no
such thing as boys' clothing, either in Europe or in its American colo-
nies. Babes-in-arms were swaddled or wore long dresses, but as soon as
a boy could walk, he wore adult clothing—but not men's. That clothing

was, for the most part, similar to women's and girls' clothing, since little boys did not wear trousers. Some of the reason was practical—attending to bathroom needs was easier in skirts for a small child—but some was cultural. Men wore pants, and babies wore dresses. But when was a boy old enough to be eligible for trousers? The answer to this question is at the center of boys' clothing in Europe and North America and in the construction of boyhood as a special category of childhood. Historian Philippe Ariès argued that "childhood" was invented as a special place for boys who were attaining masculine character and social roles but had not yet achieved manhood. A middle- or upper-class girl's path from infancy to womanhood was marked in her dress only at puberty, primarily because the traits ascribed to women—passivity, dependence, emotional and physical weakness—were also associated with infants.

The rite of passage known as "breeching," when a boy put away skirts and donned trousers, was his first step into manhood. Before the middle of the eighteenth century, boys were breeched in middle childhood, around seven or eight, and it was a watershed moment in their lives. They left the nursery for the schoolroom or left home for an apprenticeship, dressed like the adult men they were destined to become. Every article of dress was identical to that of a grown man's, which made for a dramatic transformation. This pattern shifted in the 1760s when the "skeleton suit"—the first of many intermediate styles for boys—was introduced. Skeleton suits consisted of a jacket or bodice connected with buttons to long trousers, and they were initially worn by boys between the ages of three and twelve years. They gradually went out of style by the 1830s and were replaced by an ever-changing list of styles that further distinguished early boyhood.

The prohibition against pants for girls became flexible in the nineteenth century, beginning with the introduction of underdrawers. In the 1820s, children's dresses became much shorter than women's, usually reaching to a point between the knee and the calf. This revealed the white cotton drawers, or pantalettes, which had been worn by children since around 1800. As explained in chapter 2, pantalettes, like dresses, were worn by boys as well as girls. Although a few parents preferred to cover their daughters' legs with fabric tubes rather than full-length pantalettes, underdrawers were the first bifurcated garments considered proper for girls and women.

Skeleton suit, ca. 1830. This one-piece garment features the bodice and sleeves of fashionable women's clothing.

Courtesy of the DAR Museum, Washington D.C., Friends of the Museum Purchase.

The skeleton suit and other transitional styles ushered in a convention of having distinct milestones for boys marked by changes in their wardrobe and appearance. For most of the nineteenth century until the 1920s, the first transition, from long baby clothes to short dresses, was common to both boys and girls, marking their achievement of mobility. At around age three, when their figures lost their baby roundness, boys exchanged dresses for tunics and dresses worn with wide short trousers, usually in rather fantastic styles adapted from neither women's nor men's fashions, but designed uniquely for little boys. Inspiration for these boyish styles was drawn from the more colorful and picturesque pages of men's fashion history, and ladies' magazine abounded with pictures of juvenile Romeos and cavaliers. When a boy reached school age—anywhere between five and seven—he was old enough to wear styles that were closer adaptations of men's clothing, without the ruffles, laces, and ribbons that were used in little boys' fashions. During the latter half of the nineteenth century, when long hair for boys was in vogue, this transition in clothing accompanied a boy's first short haircut. By 1905, the first haircut was more likely to coincide with the shift from dresses to short pants. So important was breeching that it appeared as a motif in children's play, in the form of "before and after" wardrobes for boy paper dolls. The Winterthur library has several of these sets, ranging from the 1870s to 1910.

The symbolic power invested in trousers was such that the transition from dresses to short pants was particularly significant. In popular sentimental literature, the baby or small boy became a "little man" at that moment. Fiction writers made much of the wrenching emotions a mother felt at seeing her boy in his first "manly" suit and haircut. The "fun" was also supposedly over in her relationship with her son. No longer his mother's baby or pet, he was now the "typical boy," proclaimed to be "an offense in himself" by an anonymous author in 1878. "It was the trousers that did it, Mary. From the time he put on trousers he has refused to kiss me," one fictional mama complained. Breeching was, similarly, partly symbolic but also partly instrumental. Dressing a boy in a more manly fashion was intended to reinforce his increasingly manly behavior. A boy's emerging masculine nature, however distressing, was not to be denied. The mother who tried to delay the inevitable was apt to end up with a spoiled, namby-pamby mama's boy, like "tiresome Mrs. Tracy" in an 1846 *Godey's* story, "with that horrid boy of hers, whom she educates at home, and takes everywhere because he is her only child."

ROMPERS: GENDERED OR NEUTRAL?

This would be a shorter, simpler chapter if the story of trousers could be confined to their adoption and use by men and boys. After the introduction of the skeleton suit in the eighteenth century, there were numerous

POLLY'S PAPER PLAYMATES.
POLLY'S BROTHER PERCY.

Next week we shall present Polly's Cousin Janet.

SUPPLEMENT TO THE BALTIMORE AMERICAN.
SUNDAY, OCTOBER 18TH, 1910.

Polly's brother Percy paper doll, 1910. His wardrobe includes skirts, tunics with knickers, and long overalls.

Courtesy of The Winterthur Library: Joseph Downs Collection of Manuscripts and Printed Ephemera.

styles for boys just below breeching age that featured short pants in a variety of styles. Between 1890 and 1910, these abbreviated styles were adopted for younger and younger boys, and by the end of the 1930s, the transition from short pants to full-length trousers had been eliminated. Throughout the twentieth century, baby boys wore dresses and nightgowns less and less, until by the 1960s boys of all ages wore pants in some form all the time. Christening gowns, the lone exception to this rule, began to be replaced with white suits with short trousers in the 1950s.

Anyone relying on the "pants are for boys" rule would have been able to correctly identify male babies and toddlers throughout the last century if this were the entire story. But the modern history of pants has a parallel narrative of their adoption by girls that challenged and complicated the rules.

Given that most children's clothing was still made at home, and the country was still years away from mass production of everyday clothing for boys and girls under six, what was the mechanism for this trend?[1] A suggestive path can be traced through early catalog descriptions, records in baby books, extant garments, and other scattered evidence. From these fragments we can assemble a sense of the rapid acceptance of some forms of pants for girls as well as boys from one to six years beginning in the 1890s. These styles included the few garments that were available ready-made (overalls, snow suits, leggings, underdrawers) and new articles of clothing made at home (creepers and rompers). In order to become acceptable for both boys and girls under the age of three, new appeals for their suitability had to override existing rules against girls wearing pants and those against infant boys wearing the quintessential masculine garment. Those appeals were to come from advice authors, parents (fathers as well as mothers), manufacturers, and even from the children themselves in their new empowered role as consumers.

The advice literature had been arguing for simpler, sturdier clothing for children since the time of Jean-Jacques Rousseau in the 1760s, with uneven success. The tides of fashion sometimes brought innovations that made it easier to run and play, but other times *la mode* would load even the smallest children down with the fabrics and trimmings of the latest women's styles. The leaders of the first women's dress reform movement, including Amelia Bloomer and Elizabeth Cady Stanton, had argued unsuccessfully for shorter dresses worn with full trousers for women in the 1850s, and the cause was revived in the 1880s. This second attempt at dress reform was more influential, coinciding synergistically with greater female participation in sports. Bloomers were common for girls' athletic wear (in the confines of a gymnasium), and various forms of trousers for women had taken over the streets with the bicycling craze of the 1890s. The leaders of the playground movement had promoted the importance of outdoor play for children since the mid-1880s. The new philosophy was that exercise should be a daily, year-round activity, except for the coldest days. In schoolyards and city parks, jungle gyms, seesaws, and swings were installed to provide boys and girls with safe places to exercise. The kindergarten movement contributed the sandbox as a play space for younger children. By the 1890s, clothes specifically designed for play were becoming popular and were available ready-made through mail-order catalogs. Both boys and girls wore overalls of denim or some other sturdy, washable fabric, warm snowsuits, and knitted leggings. It is reasonable to conclude that by the turn of the century some forms of trousers in limited settings were considered acceptable for the littlest boys and girls.

In addition to overalls and snowsuits, babies and toddlers of both sexes began to wear garments variously called creeping aprons, creepers, overalls, and rompers. The terms "creeping apron" and "creepers" appear to refer to the same loose-fitting one-piece garment with a back closure and snap-fastenings or buttons in the crotch seam to facilitate diaper changing. Creepers were intended for babies just beginning to crawl (hence the name) and were put on over their other clothing, like a pinafore with legs. This resulted in a rather comical, overstuffed appearance, as seen in the earliest evidence of creepers found in the UCLA baby books: a snapshot of a little girl born in 1904.

Rompers were a variation on this idea, but they had either a front or back closure and a waistband or belt, which was reminiscent of the earlier skeleton suit but much looser. British costume historian Clare Rose believes them to be of American origin; they first appeared in Harrods in 1910 and were not commonly worn in England until the 1920s.[2] The scant evidence available suggests that the earliest ones were homemade, possibly from commercial patterns, but they may have begun as a grassroots trend. The only American patent for a romper or creeper design, issued on June 4, 1916, to twenty-five-year-old Theodocia Bates of Sasakwa, Oklahoma, was for a significant improvement in the existing designs, consisting of the addition of knee pads. When Mrs. Bates had applied for the patent, her son Hoil was just two years old.

In the first edition (1895) of *The Care of the Baby*, prominent pediatrician John Price Crozier Griffith endorsed exercise even for babies, who should be able to wave their arms and legs without the encumbrance of long, heavy clothing. Griffith made a point of including girls in the recommendation: "Let the girl be a hoyden just as long as she pleases—the longer the better."[3] His was a leading voice for not only abandoning the long gown in favor of short dresses but also adopting creeping aprons,

Hope Jewett, about nine months, wearing a creeper. The bulkiness of the garment suggests it was worn over a dress and diaper.

Courtesy of the History and Special Collections for the Sciences, Louise M. Darling Biomedical Library, UCLA.

overalls, and rompers for all children who could crawl. The fourth edition of *The Care of the Baby* (1908) included a drawing of a creeping apron and the suggestion that overalls and rompers were an excellent choice for boys and girls up to the age of twelve months.[4] References to creepers and rompers were frequent in advice literature between 1910 and the mid-1920s. The experts were fairly consistent in their suggestions for the timing of a baby's first creepers or rompers; while the season of the year was a consideration, the general advice was that a baby needed them to protect their white dresses and allow freedom of movement.

The evidence from baby books, though sparse, suggests that not only did practice parallel the published advice but also that rompers fairly quickly replaced short dresses instead of being worn over them. Baby books did not include a prompt for "first rompers," but this information was volunteered by the parents of twenty-nine children (twenty-one boys and eight girls), sometimes in the space provided for "short clothes" and nearly always between six and twelve months of age. Robert Slade of Lexington, Kentucky (b. 1917), got his first rompers when he was nine months old:

> His Grandma made him some little rompers and he is just wild about them and so am I. I am thru with dresses for him, they don't look nice since he has started wearing the rompers.

Though not frequent, mothers' descriptions of the transition to rompers suggest that children's preferences were "heard" even when the baby was too young to speak. Consider the note by James McConnell's mother in 1915:

> His first pair of rompers were much needed at 8 months and more followed as fast as mother could make them because he wanted to be on the floor all the time. He stopped wearing dresses at 9 ½ months.

The largest mail-order company, Sears, Roebuck & Co., lagged behind the public and their advisers by a few years, but entered the market with a range of styles and price points. The 1908 catalog included "free and easy" overalls for boys and girls from one to eight years, shown on a little girl and displayed on the same page as men's work clothes. Consistent with Cook's findings regarding department store layouts, which located infant, toddler, and girls' clothing near the ladies' department and boys' outfits near the men's department, the placement of rompers in the catalogs helps us to understand the "location" of rompers in the gender landscape of the time. The Fall 1910 Sears catalog featured six styles of rompers, located in the "baby" department between the infant dresses and the girls' clothing, in three slightly different size ranges (one to five years, one to six years, and two to seven years). Generally, they were all knee-length with gathered legs and long sleeves. They buttoned down the back and featured a belt at a lowered waistline. They were available in red or blue gingham, gray stripe, and khaki (that version specifically notes that it is a "boy's or girl's romper").

The same issue contains a page of suits for "little fellows" in the "boys' department," mostly sized four through eight, but a few versions indicated they were designed for ages two and a half through six. All consisted of a long tunic or coat worn over short gathered pants.[5] The Spring 1911 catalog offered nine styles of rompers, including the six shown the previous fall plus a linen version in blue or natural, a dark blue denim, and a version available in pink or blue.[6]

In the 1910 and 1911 Sears catalogs, rompers were located in two sections: with the babies' things and in the boys' department. In both locations, they were described either as specifically for boys or for boys and girls, suggesting that rompers designed exclusively for girls did not exist. The styles for boys or girls were often given boyish names—"Little Tommy Tucker," "Little Brother," and "Honey Boy."[7] The 1910 catalog also featured a Bloomer dress for little girls with the following description:

> A capital idea. Invented by a mother for her own little girls. Waist, skirt and bloomers all in one garment; hose supporters fasten to a tab inside the belt. It is play for a child to dress herself alone, as the dress can be put on or taken off in a moment's time. By stepping in the bloomers, slipping her arms inside the sleeves, then buttoning a few buttons, the child is dressed. It reduces the washing for the child to one-half.[8]

Sears did not offer "creepers" or rompers sized six months to two years until its Spring 1913 catalog, nearly a decade after Hope Jewett toddled in hers. These smaller versions were available in blue denim or pink or blue chambray, in the same section of the catalog as the short white dresses.[9]

From the beginning, Sears devoted separate sections to rompers for boys up to the age of six or seven and rompers for girls and boys under two years. Initially, these did not differ greatly in style, color, fabric, or trim, but just duplicated the offerings in the baby section. This appears to shift during the 1920s, as gender symbolism is added to differentiate between boys' and girls' styles. The assembled layettes—collections of "necessities" sold as a unit—never included creepers or rompers, while white dresses persisted in layettes through the late 1950s, which suggests that, despite their popularity, rompers never achieved the status of a newborn's wardrobe basic. One reason for this might be that they quickly became fashion items, with so many stylistic variations that their selection was best left up to the individual consumer, whether parent, relative, or friend. By contrast, by the 1920s, the short white dress had become a fossilized item that changed very little over the next few decades.

Paper dolls of the period give us some sense of the extent to which rompers were gendered. One of the more popular types of paper dolls was the "brother-sister" set, with matching or coordinated outfits. One particularly detailed series, by artist Sheila Young, appeared between 1919 and 1921 in *Good Housekeeping* magazine and featured a school-age girl, Polly Pratt, and her various friends, including two sets of boy-girl twins. In one of these sets, only the girl twin wears rompers; her brother is given a button-on suit (an updated version of the skeleton suit, but with short trousers) and two outfits consisting of a smock or tunic worn over short pants. In the other set, they wear matching rompers, but the girl's closes in the back and the boy's has buttons in front. This aligns with other evidence that rompers may have gradually become a feminized garment, associated with babies of both sexes and older girls. An internet search on "rompers" today retrieves images of grown women wearing short, one-piece garments with elasticized leg openings, a style that goes back to gym suits and beachwear from the 1930s. Patterns for children's rompers from the 1950s and after also suggest that they were considered suitable only for boys under one year old, not for toddlers and preschoolers.

Alternative trousered styles for little boys appeared almost at the same time as rompers themselves. In the 1908 edition of *The Care of the Child,* John Griffith hesitated to dictate "the time and manner of show-ing the difference of sex by the dress," but he offered a few suggestions for parents wishing guidance in that direction: Around the age of two, "depending on the size of the child," boys should wear dresses with box pleats from the neck and a belt or a Russian blouse suit for boys, while the "baby dress," gathered in a yoke, was preferred for girls. At three or four, "depending on the size and shape of the child and the wish of the parents," the boy could be put into trousers, either knickerbockers or the popular sailor costume.[10] Based on photographic and artifact evidence, and the size ranges for those outfits in mail-order catalogs, boys were likely to transition from rompers to other styles earlier than Griffith sug-gests, between one and two years and not much later.

Brother-sister paper dolls of the period from 1920 to 1940 give some idea of the various ways in which rompers, bloomers, and other trouser forms could be worn by boys and girls. Dolly Dingle's friend Janet and her brother Jackie (1922) were both dressed in gingham—Janet in a pink dress with bloomers, Jackie in lavender-blue rompers. Joan and Bobby

(1928) were given coordinated outfits (but not identical). Joan's blue dress has a round collar trimmed with narrow braid, while Bobby's blue romper has a ruffled collar and cuffs. Twins Punch and Judy, appearing in *Woman's Home Companion* from November 1923 through July 1924, offer a particularly valuable window into age- and gender-appropriate fashions in the mid-1920s, because they aged from one to six years in the course of those months. At one and two they are physically alike, with identical rompers and smock-and-shorts outfits in different colors. By the time they are six, their outfits are the same colors but in different styles; for example, Judy wears an orange middy with navy bloomers and Punch has a blue middy with orange shorts. Homemade clothing for the same set at the Winterthur Library consists of bloomer dresses for two-year-old Judy and coordinated rompers for Punch, with the same trimming and collars.

In the paper doll sets, pink and blue are used for "his and hers" versions for a few outfits, but not in a consistent pattern. There are also several matching pink and matching blue outfits. Dresses and one-piece rompers were more common for girls and for very little boys, while dresses featuring matching visible panties were for girls only. Not all paper dolls followed this pattern. The paper doll wardrobe of Betty Bob's baby brother, Bobby, with two dresses, one romper, and one button-on suit, seems unusual for its 1925 publication date, as are Bobby's long golden ringlets.[11] By that date, boys' outfits were more likely to be button-on suits or to feature a smock or blouse worn over loose shorts. Also popular for formal events was the Eton suit with its short jacket, paired with a fancy shirt.

The button-on suit appears to have been introduced around the same time as rompers, between 1900 and 1910. It resembles the skeleton suit of the late eighteenth and early nineteenth century, but with short trousers and a looser fit. Together with the sailor suit, the button-on suit became a perennial favorite for little boys who had outgrown dresses, particularly for festive occasions. The winter "holiday" version was often made up in black or red velveteen; the spring model could be short-sleeved or even sleeveless and constructed of pastel or white linen or cotton.

The number of dresses listed in the baby books as gifts for boys declined as rompers became more common. Still there were outliers on each extreme: Henry Jay Van de Weg of Grand Rapids, Michigan, was baptized wearing "a little blue romper" in 1940, well in advance of the

Baby Brother Bob paper doll, 1920. His wardrobe includes rompers, dresses (some with matching bloomers), and a button-on suit.

Courtesy, The Winterthur Library: Joseph Downs Collection of Manuscripts and Printed Ephemera.

decline of the christening gown, and William Perry Smith Jr. of Sanford, Florida (b. 1945), traded dresses for his first rompers at two months, very late for that time.

The introduction of rompers and creepers complicates our interpretation of the use of two-legged, or bifurcated, garments for babies and very young children. Consider a blue gingham romper from 1910, which could have been worn by either a one-year-old boy or girl, but for different reasons. The boy's parents might have chosen the romper as a way to encourage masculine identity, while putting his sister in dresses at the same age. Parents of a girl could have dressed her in a romper to encourage her to be physically active, and then handed it down to a little brother for the same practical reason. Edna Alverson's baby book included not only a snapshot of her wearing rompers at four (in 1920) but also her mother wearing a knickers suit at around the same time, indicating that in the Alverson household, everyone wore pants. Without knowing the tastes and preferences of a particular family, manufacturers and retailers had to allow for many possible options when deciding on fabrics and merchandising. Perhaps it was this uncertainty that kept the design of rompers neutral for the first ten or fifteen years. By the 1920s, gender distinctions were becoming more common in rompers and other trouser forms for play, moving them out of the neutral category and steadily into the "feminine" side of the wardrobe.

Similarly, distinctive masculine and feminine creeper styles for infants began to appear in the mail-order catalogs in the 1920s, while the industry discussion about the preferred gender significance of pink and blue continued well into the 1930s. Neutral styles remained an important part of the infant wear market, however; babies grew rapidly, and clothes that could be handed down to the next child were more practical than gendered clothing through the restrictions of the Great Depression and World War II.

Girls' play clothes have featured a growing variety of trouser styles since the early twentieth century: shorts, jeans, capris, and overalls, just to name a few. Their practical nature tended to argue against the use of elaborate trims and decoration, so that styles plain enough to be neutral were still plentiful. As was the case for older girls and women, less casual versions for school, church, or festive occasions did not begin to gain broad acceptance until the late 1960s, with the influence of unisex fashions. Since 1985, girls' trouser styles have become more feminine in appearance, and it is reasonable to say that pants have long since ceased to be a "masculine" garment.

Between 1890 and the end of World War I, American children's clothing had undergone a dramatic transformation. Like adult fashions (especially women's) clothing, it had become simpler in cut, less fussy

Edna Alverson, age four, in her rompers. The unfastened belt is visible hanging on her right side.

in decoration, and less restrictive. Evidently these changes were the responses to the same external factors sweeping through the rest of the
industrialized world: a revolution in the manufacture and distribution
of clothing, rising consumerism, and less formal use of leisure time. But
some of the innovations in children's fashions suggest changes more
closely tied to more specifically gender-related concerns. These concerns
stemmed directly from parents' hopes and worries about their children's
sexual and gender identities, but also express their own anxieties about
traditional and emerging gender expectations. The introduction, acceptance, and eventual gendering of shorts, rompers, and other forms of
trousers are a material record of these anxieties. Philippe Ariès noted the
realization of the child's soul and individual agency in depictions of children in sixteenth-century portraits; Sigmund Freud introduced the idea
that very early experiences—even in infancy—unconsciously shape our
adult natures, particularly our sexual desires. The popular spread of these
ideas led parents to the inevitable conclusion that little children must also
have gender, but it left unanswered the questions of when they "have it"
and how it should be expressed.

Clothing manufacturers and retailers harnessed the expertise of
child development professionals to provide material solutions to parental fears. The child consumer—an artifact of marketing, not a real boy or
girl[12]—had needs and wants which parents did not always comprehend
but which had to be translated by helpful advice, fashion, and advertising copywriters. The growing child needed rompers and other trousered
play clothes in order to develop a strong body and to play freely, without
concerns about spoiling delicate or elaborate clothing. This need for freedom was extended to girls as well as boys and to younger and younger
infants. Instead of observing a calendar of sartorial transitions for their
sons—short dresses at six months, tunics with short trousers at three,
knickers at seven, and long trousers at twelve—parents were advised to
look for signs of readiness. These might include increased mobility or
insistence on being treated less like a baby and more like "a little man."
Developmentally, this would be likely to happen in the third year. Girls
who were active and "hoydenish" also needed play clothes that permitted
movement and allowed them to get dirty, and parents were reassured that
this would be a stage and that even their little tomboy would eventually
begin to pine for pretty frocks and quieter pastimes.

It is not clear from the artifactual record that the advice givers were
able to completely dispel parental fears. What about "gentle" boys? Boys

who were small or delicate-looking and frequently mistaken for girls? Girls so "boyish" they could not be coaxed into dresses? Wouldn't dressing boys and girls differently draw their attention to sex differences before parents were ready to explain them? Did wearing pants encourage masturbation? Anxious tension between maintaining their children's innocence and guaranteeing normal sexual development, all the while nurturing their individuality, complicated the adoption of pants by girls, the earlier adoption of pants by boys, and the emergence of feminine trouser styles.

If the present scene was just a continuation of the late nineteenth century, with the addition of rompers for practical reasons only, rompers and white infant dresses would still exist, perhaps with dresses for newborns and dressy occasions and rompers for play. Both rompers and dresses would be considered neutral, just appropriate for different occasions. Toddlers, older girls, and women would wear trousered styles only for sports and active play and seldom in public. What happened instead was a tug-of-war between neutral and gendered bifurcated styles, with the scales tilting over time toward gendered versions of pants. Much of this negotiation took place between 1920 and 1940, as colors, motifs, and other details were gradually sorted into "his" and "hers" categories. While pants today are for boys *and* girls, most are designed to make the distinction crystal clear.

A BOY IS NOT A GIRL

What are little boys made of, made of?
What are little boys made of?
Snips and snails and puppy dogs tails;
And such are little boys made of.

What are little girls made of, made of?
What are little girls made of?
Sugar and spice and everything nice;
That's what little girls are made of.

THIS OLD ENGLISH NURSERY RHYME, dating to around 1820, is a reminder that, even as babies were believed to lack masculinity and femininity, slightly older boys and girls were perceived as gendered beings with very different character traits. The mystery to their parents (and the puzzle to historians) is how a tiny, ungendered cherub came to prefer "snips and snails" to "sugar and spice." The decline of white baby dresses and the introduction of rompers are the first two parts of the puzzle, altering established patterns of children's clothing and challenging existing notions of how and when children acquire gender identity. The third transformation took place in parallel with those changes, but focused just on boys and the apparently sudden urgency of distinguishing them from girls earlier and earlier.

The long tradition of dressing boys and girls alike seems curiously inappropriate to modern eyes. American babies in the twenty-first century are gendered, named, and furnished with appropriate clothing, room décor, and toys months before birth, and they are only perceived as neutral for the very first weeks of pregnancy. Understanding the history of today's "little man" model of boys' wear requires untangling and reconnecting three narratives. First, there is the rise and eventual fall of the Little Lord Fauntleroy suit, which went from nationwide craze to anathema between 1885 and 1900. Second, there is the shift in beliefs about the role of sexual identity in infant and early child development, driven by the rise of the academic field of psychology in America. Together, the Fauntleroy suit and the influence of child psychology turned traditional wisdom about gender-appropriate children's clothing on its head between 1900 and 1920. Finally, there is the protracted negotiation of gender symbolism in the children's clothing market, which resulted in the purging of "feminine" details from little boys' clothing by the late 1940s.[1]

The net impact of these three transitions was to justify, clarify, and solidify the conviction that masculinity was inherent in baby boys, but in a fragile form that required protection and reinforcement. The cherubic white dresses of infancy, once worn well into the third year, shifted in less than a generation from being exactly right for babies to not only wrong but harmful for boys. A boy was not a girl and should never be mistaken for a girl. Banishing white dresses was just the beginning; lace, ruffles, gathers, flowers, kittens, and a sizable portion of the color spectrum were all eliminated from little boys' clothing over the course of several decades. Replacing them were the emblems of masculinity: sports motifs, military details, and machines, such as cars, trucks, trains, and airplanes, all clearly signifying *boy*, not *girl*.

Histories of the Victorian era are rich with descriptions of men's public exploits and accomplishments, and scholars of masculinity studies have shed considerable light on the private, individual experience of being male. But as with childhood in general, the very early years of boyhood can only be understood indirectly. By examining fashions for infants and toddler boys during the period, we can begin to understand the social conventions that guided them, the limits of their self-expression, and the expectations that they faced. Adult reminiscences, when available, can be helpful as well, although the earliest months and years of life remain inaccessible. A third, generational approach is used in this chapter: considering dramatic changes in children's culture to be not only the product of their own times but a very delayed reaction to significant events or trends in the childhood of contemporary adults. The example of the Fauntleroy suit—treated not only as an important trend in its own time (1889–95) but also as a significant motivator for trends fifteen to twenty years later—occupies a large portion of this chapter for that reason.

"THE RULES" FOR BOYS BEFORE
LITTLE LORD FAUNTLEROY

When clothing for babies was mainly neutral, the first visual distinction between boys and girls—skeleton suits or other boys' styles—was
not made until they were in their second year at the earliest. Knowing
when a boy was "old enough" to dress less like a girl and more like a
boy (if not yet like a little man) was not easy, as region, class, and other
variables dictated the transition, in addition to the boy's own appearance
and personality. The second, more dramatic distinction in boys' fashions,
between little boys and older boys, was more likely to be based on age or
entry into school than on the boy himself, at least in the nineteenth century. This reflected the popular understanding of gender identity acquisition as gradually emerging consciousness from babyhood through early
childhood, to which parents should respond with restraint.

Published advice for most of the 1800s cautioned against putting
boys in any form of trousers too early, for a variety of reasons. Early in
the century, the most common rationale was that dresses provided more
freedom than the tight jackets and trousers of the period. Curiously, the
loudest advocates of this position were authors such as William Alcott (b.
1798) and William Dewees (b. 1768), who were likely to have worn skeleton suits as children.[2] It is worth considering that while adults had hailed
skeleton suits as a better option than men's fashions for boys, those who
wore them remembered the experience differently. In an essay published
in 1836, Charles Dickens (b. 1812) characterized a skeleton suit as "one
of those straight blue cloth cases in which small boys used to be confined,
before belts and tunics had come in."[3] Each of these authors, writing in
the mid-1830s, expressed approval of the loose tunics or dresses for little
boys coming into fashion at the time.

Boys and girls wore identical or very similar dress styles until the age
of four or five until midcentury, when picturesque fashions for boys made
their appearance. According to *Godey's Magazine and Lady's Book,* short
loose trousers were permitted for "boys between dresses and pantaloons"
(August 1852) when worn beneath dresses or long tunics (December
1856). Dress styles for boys and girls were essentially similar, sometimes
with less trim for boys, though what constituted "less trim" in the 1870s
and 1880s was far from plain in the modern sense. In portraits, photographs, and fashion illustrations, the only reliable clue to a child's gender

is pants. The picturesque styles drew from exotic, historical, or military fashions for men—Scottish kilts, sailor suits, Zouave jackets, "Romeo" tunics, and cavalier suits based on seventeenth-century models—and were offered as a way to introduce masculine styling without dressing a small boy just like a grown man. They also complemented women's fashions of the day and trends in interior decorations.

The age of transition from baby dresses to little boy styles dipped slightly after 1850, from ages four or five to three or four. In practice, the change could be made whenever the boy grew too tall for his baby dresses; instead of making longer dresses as she would for a girl, the mother took his first growth spurt as her cue to change his wardrobe. The next shift, to knickerbockers or other short trousers worn with more tailored shirts and jackets, took place when the boy lost his "baby appearance" around five or six. With the rules so vaguely sketched and based on subjective judgments by parents, it is hard to imagine that all boys moved from dresses to tunic suits and from tunic suits to knickerbockers based on rigid conventions rather than their parents' sentiments.

The educational role of clothing, and its usefulness in conveying important moral values, was a significant part of nineteenth-century advice literature for mothers. Freedom to move and play was to be a primary consideration for little boys and girls, with the understanding that they would enjoy less liberty as adults. The advice literature set forth general principles, but offered few details or examples. Mothers were cautioned not to dress their children too richly or elaborately or to teach them to value clothing too highly: "It is bad enough to teach girls to be vain, but boys—awful!" wrote an anonymous author in *Godey's* in October 1854. Vanity was seen as a natural inclination of all children, a vice to be moderated in girls and eliminated in boys.

"THE FAUNTLEROY PLAGUE"

Men's fashionable clothing had once equaled or excelled that of women. In the fifteenth century, Henry VIII of England was an arbiter of taste and style in his famous portraits: velvet, lace, jewels, fur, all elaborately and exuberantly designed to convey his wealth and power as a monarch and as a man. Or consider the visibility of George Washington's well-turned calves, encased in embroidered silk stockings—in contrast to women's invisible and, in polite society, unmentionable appendages.

England's famous Regency dandy, Beau Brummell, popularized a style that was less flamboyant but no less intentional in its sensual embrace of fine fabrics, starched linen, and careful arrangement of the tiniest detail. Until well after the Civil War, American men could wear elaborate vests, brightly colored shirts, and shoulder-length hair without ever giving a thought to looking "feminine." The last two decades of the nineteenth century were years of tremendous change in American men's fashion. Men's clothing had been undergoing a gradual evolution from colorful, individualistic, and expressive to drab, conformist, and utilitarian, an evolution which dress historians trace back to the seventeenth-century Puritan styles in England, with their rejection of ostentation and display. The acceptance of the boxy, practical sack suit for everyday business dress, accomplished during the 1880s, opened the final act in a drama that had been playing out for at least two hundred years. Darwin's theory of natural selection, paired with the work of early ethnographers, advanced the belief that modern clothing, with its sharp distinctions between men and women, was a hallmark of advanced civilization. Middle- and upper-class "western" men's plain, utilitarian clothing was evidence of their superiority to less evolved cultures, inferior races, and lower-class men and women in general. Adult desire for color, decoration, and novelty was generalized as "effeminate" or "degenerate" across class lines. Children's desire for lively colors and patterns was further proof of this evolutionary theory, because it demonstrated their similarity to "primitive" peoples.

If scientific evidence had not been sufficient to persuade men to replace the older, occasion-specific styles with the sack suit for business dress, there was also the considerable influence of popular humor. During the 1880s, weekly humor magazines such as *Puck, Judge,* and *Life* published dozens of cartoons featuring foolish, foppish creatures known as "dudes." Dudes were instantly identifiable by their dress, which included monocles, walking sticks, and fastidiously correct, occasion-specific suits. No dude ever wore a sack suit. By the 1880s, the sack suit was well established as the uniform of the go-getter, the man of the coming century, and the older styles were identified in hundreds of popular caricatures with dudes, politicians, and members of the genteel poor, such as college professors and clergymen.[4]

Boys' fashions had also been transformed since the late eighteenth century, with the introduction of the skeleton suit and other trousered styles for boys too young for men's clothing. While these changes were sometimes related to men's clothing trends, they did not appear at the same time, nor did they proceed at the same rate. They were, in fact, the manifestations of two cultural norms that existed in tension with each other: a boy is not a man, and a man is not a woman. The first expresses the strong age-related conventions, which translated into attempts to establish and maintain boundaries between childhood and adulthood, as well as into elaborate styles for boys between two and seven. The distinctions between men and women, though always present in status and everyday interactions, were rapidly drawn more visibly after the Civil War, as men's clothing became plainer and simpler in cut. These two trends—plainer dress for men and fancy dress for little boys—collided in the late 1880s when the Little Lord Fauntleroy craze burst onto the scene.

At the same time that American men were exchanging lively patterns and colors for plain broadcloth and worsted suits and vests, their sons and younger brothers were being measured for Little Lord Fauntleroy suits, thanks to the remarkable popularity of a story by Frances Hodgson Burnett. *Little Lord Fauntleroy* was originally published as a serial in *St. Nicholas,* a children's magazine, in 1886; a book version appeared the same year. The serialized story and the book enjoyed great success. Translated into twelve languages and selling over a million copies in English alone, by 1893 *Little Lord Fauntleroy* could be found on the shelves of 72 percent of America's public libraries, second only to *Ben Hur.*[5]

Burnett told the sentimental tale of an American boy, Cedric Errol, and his widowed mother, who are summoned to England so that Cedric may meet his paternal grandfather and take his rightful place as Lord Fauntleroy, heir to his grandfather's estate. The old Earl dislikes Americans and refuses to meet his American daughter-in-law, insisting that the boy live with him, apart from his beloved mother. Gradually, the Earl discovers that Cedric is a courageous, chivalrous boy with a strong sense of right and duty, due mainly to the influence of his American mother, who is finally allowed to rejoin Cedric and enjoy the love and respect of her father-in-law.

Although he was dressed in the picturesque styles of the day, Cedric was no dude in miniature. Cedric's physical appearance and dress were an outward sign of his own natural nobility, as well as his mother's efforts to raise him as a gentleman, despite her straitened circumstances. Burnett introduced seven-year-old Cedric running breathlessly down the New York streets, described in the words of a devoted servant: "An' ivvery man,

Boy, age three or four, in a Fauntleroy suit, 1898.

Courtesy of the History and Special Collections for the Sciences, Louise M. Darling Biomedical Library, UCLA.

woman and child lookin' afther him in his bit of black velvet skirt made out of the misthress's ould gound."[6] Later, Cedric wins a footrace wearing a cream-colored flannel suit with a red sash, his long golden locks streaming behind them. There was nothing novel about the styles worn by Cedric Errol—velvet "cavalier" suits and white wool flannel suits with brightly colored sashes had been fashionable for some time. Nor was his long hair remarkable; at seven, his first haircut was just around the corner, and no one would have looked askance at a little boy in a velvet suit and shoulder-length hair. It is probably accurate to say that thousands of American boys were already dressing like Little Lord Fauntleroy at the time the story was published. Certainly one was: an 1885 photograph of the author's seven-year-old son, Vivian Burnett, in his velvet cavalier suit was sent to illustrator Reginald Birch as a model for his drawings of Cedric Errol. The velvet suits worn by Vivian and his older brother, Lionel, were similar to dressy outfits that had been acceptable fashions for middle-class boys for at least a generation.

Peterson's Magazine described the following outfit in 1865, more than twenty years before the publication of *Little Lord Fauntleroy*: "A little boy's knickerbocker suit of black velvet. It is trimmed with fur and fastened at the waist with a belt of leather. Black velvet cap." During the 1880s, seventeenth-century-style black velvet suits with long jackets, knee breeches, and matching vests, often called cavalier suits, were among the most popular styles for boys from the ages of four to seven or eight. The common practice of postponing the first haircut as long as possible enhanced the picturesque period effect, transforming the boy into a miniature D'Artagnan.

The impact of Burnett's book might have been minimal, were it not for the stage adaptation, which brought the story to life for audiences across the United States. Burnett herself wrote the play and made a considerable amount of money from the venture, despite a disagreement with her publisher and producer over who controlled a property that the *New York Times* called "more valuable than any other on the American stage."[7] The play opened in London in May 1888, previewed in Boston in September, and moved to Broadway in December.[8] A *New York Times* reviewer wrote, after seeing the preview, "As an ideal picture of childlife as 'Little Lord Fauntleroy' has never been sup-posed."[9] As was the common practice, little girls were often cast in the children's roles. Of child actress Elsie Leslie, the first of many girls to portray Cedric, a reviewer for *Peterson's Magazine* wrote, "She is a lovely figure in Cedric's dainty costumes and her photograph in character will be in the shop windows before too long." The same writer continued, "Every mother will like the pretty play, the children will be taken to see it, and few fathers will object to it."[10]

Many children were indeed taken to see it; most audiences included large numbers of children, a phenomenon that more than one reviewer noted. *Little Lord Fauntleroy* was claimed to be the first play written for children and the first to make extensive use of child actors, for Cedric was not the only juvenile part. By the spring of 1889, the "Fauntleroy" mania had spread throughout the country. In June, there were two New York productions, three companies in Boston, and two in Chicago, in addition to at least a dozen more touring companies. Eventually *Little Lord Fauntleroy* played for nearly four years in New York and two years in London.

Of course, what *Little Lord Fauntleroy* did for the cavalier suit was associate it with a wildly popular "brand" of fictional hero and give it new life—and a new name. The Fauntleroy suit enjoyed its greatest popularity in the fall and winter of 1889–90, after the play had reached audiences all over the country. *Godey's Magazine and Lady's Book* provided a very good description of the style in September 1889: "For small boys nothing has met with such universal favor as the Fauntleroy suit. It certainly is the most attractive seen for some time. It is usually made of black velvet or velveteen, with a broad collar and cuffs of Irish point lace, with a sash of silk passed broadly around the waist and knotted on one side." *Peterson's Magazine* showed another version in green velvet in February 1890. Fauntleroy suits continued to appear for several years, although by the fall of 1890 they were often listed after the increasingly popular middy (or sailor) suits and Norfolk jackets. They were usually described as being suitable for boys from three to eight, with skirted versions sometimes offered for the youngest boys.

The Fauntleroy suit was not really "universally favored," as *Godey's* claimed. Even fans of the book could see that Cedric's attraction was not universal; *St. Nicholas* published a letter from an eighteen-year-old female reader who had "fallen in love with Little Lord Fauntleroy": "I wish the 'small boy' of the present day would copy after him, but I fear that would be too 'pretty a state of things.'"[11] It's very likely that Burnett's fans were women and girls rather than boys or men. When the *New York Times*

Harvey Fell, age four or five, wearing a sailor tunic
over knickers and dark leggings, about 1915.
University of Maryland Costume and Textile Collection.

polled 400 boys in 1895 about the best books for children, the list included *Ivanhoe, The Three Musketeers,* and several works by Dickens—but no
Little Lord Fauntleroy, despite the thousands of copies that had been sold.
Some literary critics were positive and complimentary—Arthur Bartlett
Maurice in *Bookman* attributed the tale's popularity to the timeless theme
of virtue rewarded and Cedric's Cinderella-like journey from poverty to
wealth.[12] But an anonymous reviewer in 1906, while acknowledging the

appeal of redemptive child figures, contrasted Cedric Errol with David, a character in Mrs. Deland's *Awakening of Helena Richie*. David is a "perfectly natural, uncoddled, and healthy boy," "free from the hectic glow of cloistered or unusual childhood."[13]

The literary figures most often contrasted with Cedric Errol were Tom Sawyer and Huckleberry Finn. Huck first appeared in Mark Twain's 1876 *Adventures of Tom Sawyer* and took center stage in his own story, *The Adventures of Huckleberry Finn,* published in the United States in 1885—the same year *Little Lord Fauntleroy* was originally serialized in *St. Nicholas*. Dan Beard, founder of the Boys Scouts of America, noted in 1904, "In America, it is the Huck Finns and Tom Sawyers who mature into healthy, wholesome men, and not the degenerate little Lord Fauntleroys."[14] Beard, born in 1850, had married in 1892 and by 1904 was the father of a son, Daniel Bartlett Beard, who, one suspects, probably did not dress in velvet cavalier suits.

By 1895, the Fauntleroy craze showed signs of subsiding; although the style remained in circulation, boys' fashions began to undergo changes that echoed what had occurred in men's dress, only much more rapidly. Skirted and even knickerbocker styles for preschoolers fell into disuse, as boys were put into shorts or knee breeches as early as one or two years of age. The sailor blouse, paired with knickers, short pants, or trousers, won favor with many families as a dressy outfit for family portraits or parties.[15] Considering the direction of men's fashions in the 1880s and the rapid transformation of boys' clothing after 1895, it is quite possible that the Fauntleroy suit was responsible for accelerating the revolution.

The boys of America had not been polled about the desirability of cavalier suits, nor had their fathers, and both groups were now influencing the marketplace. Resistance to Fauntleroy suits appeared almost as soon as they were introduced, particularly from school-age boys, who, in the words of John Nicholas Beffel, "stood midway between Huck Finn and Little Lord Fauntleroy and suddenly they were herded towards the latter."[16] Newspapers carried occasional, unsubstantiated rumors of boys deliberately ruining their velvet finery, or of getting into fights after being ridiculed by other boys, in an interesting echo of accusations of "dudeism" among men at the same time. Beffel also tells the story of an eight-year-old in Davenport, Iowa, in 1889 who burned down his family's barn because he was forced to wear a Little Lord Fauntleroy suit. This is an extreme example (and possibly apocryphal) but still an indicator of the largely unrecorded resentment many boys felt about the style. In these stories, the boys are usually six or older; younger boys may have been sheltered from similar embarrassment by their less public lives, but the proliferation of photographic portraits at the end of the century guaranteed that their ringlets and charming costumes would be displayed in the parlor for years after they had been outgrown.

Strong evidence for this notion of the role of fathers in the fate of Little Lord Fauntleroy is what happened to his reputation when the boys of the 1880s reached manhood. Plucky, manly Cedric Errol became transformed into a sissy. The term "Little Lord Fauntleroy" became synonymous with a pretty, effeminate mamma's boy. In a *New York Times Magazine* article published shortly after Burnett's death, an anonymous author asked, "What would a modern boy think about Little Lord Fauntleroy?" He imagines that the boy of 1924 would have the same reaction as most boys in 1888, quoting Tom Sawyer upon encountering a "citified" boy in "natty" clothes: "I can lick you."[17]

The essay's author provides additional perspective on the style, presumably that of a former Fauntleroy-suffering boy. Part of the problem was that "fond mamas did not choke off their baby Galahads at the end of the chapter but kept right on," suggesting that boys as old as twelve suffered the indignities of velvet suits and flowing curls. One slight benefit of the style, in the author's opinion, was that boys in Fauntleroy suits had to defend themselves because of their appearance, which made them tougher. The boy of 1924 lived in a different world, he claimed, filled with scientific marvels, emancipated women, and sex-saturated media. Boys of six or seven no longer had to sneak off to the barber for their first haircuts but were taken as toddlers by their bobbed-haired sisters or mothers. Even Cedric's devotion to his mother was disturbing to modern readers; their relationship "was very much the kind for which later psychiatrists have invented special names," alluding to "momism," the overattachment that Freudian psychologists believed led to sexual dysfunction or perversion.

John Nicholas Beffel's 1927 essay "The Fauntleroy Plague" offers modern readers some insight into the Fauntleroy experience from a child's point of view. It is a striking departure from most of Beffel's work—he was a radical journalist best known for his coverage of the Sacco-Vanzetti trial in 1915. But Beffel was also born in 1887, just in time to experience the full force of the Fauntleroy craze. The inspiration for his essay was the news that the Manhattan park commissioners had rejected the Burnett monument proposed for Central Park. The ostensible reason for their decision was lack of space and too many monuments in the popular park. Beffel suggests the real reason was because "among the commissioners is one man, or more than one, who in his day was a victim of the Fauntleroy plague."

In his scathing essay, Beffel located the craze between 1889 and 1899 and observed that "great numbers were seen at the World's Fair in 1892." He accurately described the style as "the vogue of long curls, velvet jacket and pants, lace collar and cuffs and velvet tam-o'-shanter" and labeled the book and play's popularity "incredible," considering that Cedric "looked like a girl and was played by a girl" in the original play. Moreover, he argued, the aristocratic, cavalier style was out of place in republican America, with its "rough and ready" youngsters for whom the fussy outfit was "a straitjacket a psychological wall between them and freedom of spirit." "No self-respecting boy," he wrote "likes to be spoken of as beautiful."

The Fauntleroy suit also underwent an interesting change in definition. In 1889, the name denoted a very specific style, made of velvet and distinguished by a lace collar and a broad sash. By 1910, the term was used to describe velvet suits in general, and eventually it became a generic label for dressy boys' suits with fancy collars. Interviews conducted with men in their seventies in 1991 found that some even referred to fancy sailor suits of the World War I era as "Fauntleroy suits" or, in one case, "those damn Fauntleroy suits."[18] The Burnett character and the clothes he inspired provided a focal point for the rejection of picturesque clothing for boys, in the same way that the dude helped bring about the demise of occasion-specific dress for men.

One important distinction between Little Lord Fauntleroy and the dude needs to be made: their creators' intentions. The dude was a ridiculous stereotype of the fashionable man from the very start. In contrast, Frances Hodgson Burnett—and evidently many of her readers—saw Cedric Errol as the perfect son. The fans of the book and the play appear to have been predominantly female—and small wonder. *Little Lord Fauntleroy* is very much the story of a boy's devotion to his mother and the power of a mother's influence on her child. It was mothers, according to the press, who brought their children to see the play, and mothers who purchased or created velvet suits for their own sons. Scattered articles in women's magazines, beginning around 1905, suggested that the trend toward more masculine dress for little boys came about due to pressure from fathers, who objected to styles that were too feminine. Given the twenty-year span since the "Lord Fauntleroy plague," it could very well be that the survivors of that fancy dress style finally had their say.

With their own sartorial questions settled with the acceptance of the business suit, men may have understood more clearly than women what to make of boys' clothing in the coming century. The Fauntleroy craze, which at an earlier time would have been just one more brief fashion, was instead the last straw. Unknowingly, Frances Hodgson Burnett may have provided the catalyst that helped translate the new image of American man into the more masculine image of the American boy.

The new American boyhood demanded a change in image to reflect the growing emphasis on athleticism, physical fitness, and gender. The picturesque costumes of the 1870s and 1880s had left their mark on the parents of the turn of the century, who rejected such finery for their own children, especially their sons. At times the Little Lord Fauntleroy suit was named specifically, accused of turning a boy into "a caricature" and attracting bullies to prey on him. A thoughtful mother would not exhibit her son in picturesque costumes to her visitors as if he were an exotic pet, but instead would provide him with comfortable, sturdy, and inconspicuous play clothes. In the same way that mothers were seen as proxy consumers for babies until they were old enough to make their own preferences known, fathers were enlisted to advocate for their sons, particularly when mothers wanted to make Fauntleroys of them. It is no accident that this rejection of picturesque styles coincided with the adulthood of the very boys who had endured the brunt of the Fauntleroy craze, proof that the child is, indeed, father to the man.

CHILD PSYCHOLOGY AND BOY-RAISING

The rise and fall of the Fauntleroy suit occurred just as the academic field of psychology was beginning to influence medical professionals and educated parents in the United States. The findings of child psychologists, led by the prolific and influential scholar G. Stanley Hall, were translated into advice in newspapers, journals, magazines, and books. The new experts routinely compared the "modern" white, middle-class American children with their counterparts of earlier generations, lower classes, and "inferior" races. In this light, white middle-class children were seen to be at risk in the new century, and with them, the future of the nation.

American boys were the focus of most of the concern about the next generation. Girls, it seemed, were already well on their way to becoming the new women of the twentieth century. The advent of both coeducational colleges and women's colleges with rigorous liberal arts programs was helping to dispel long held beliefs about the educability of women. Feminists had been promoting the benefits of sports and exercise for girls and women for years. By the turn of the century, popular opinion shifted to become more accepting of active sports for girls and young women. Many writers noted with obvious approval that young women of the 1890s were better educated, more independent, and healthier than women of their mothers' generation. Their clothing was beginning to reflect these changes, being less restrictive, more practical, and less elaborate, at least in the case of everyday dress. Women were even beginning to adopt trousers, in the form of bloomers or divided skirts, for sports such as bicycling. To a scientific community already pondering the implications of Darwin's work on evolution, women's apparently successful adaptation to meet the demands of the new millennium raised concerns: What would happen if men did not progress at the same pace? What if the emergence of strong women foreshadowed the decline of male power and domination? The survival of the species seemed to demand a fit companion to the new woman: a new, tougher go-getter of a man. Instead, according to their research, middle-class white boys were becoming getting weaker, lazier, less healthy, and more inclined to sexual "depravity," particularly masturbation and homosexuality.

American boys became the target of a massive rehabilitation effort. The introduction of team sports in public schools dates from this period, as do the Boy Scouts of America. Articles and books on raising boys proliferated. *Harper's Bazaar* ran a regular column in 1910 entitled "The Question of the Boy." William McKeever, a professor at the Kansas Agricultural College, now Kansas State University, published a series of pamphlets on raising boys that reached nearly 16 million copies between 1908 and 1911.[19] The pamphlets, based on the model of agricultural experiment station bulletins on livestock, included titles such as "The Cigarette Smoking Boy," "Teaching the Boy to Work," and "Assisting the Boy in the Choice of a Vocation." The experts' prescription was clear: rigorous exercise, chores or other work, and as much schooling as possible to encourage healthy development. In the *Ladies' Home Journal* article "How We Trained Our Boy," one father explained his successful techniques for child rearing that included using a Spartan regime of cold baths, daily exercise (a punching bag, beginning at age five), and an increasing load of household chores.

In the 1880s, G. Stanley Hall had published the first of many scholarly and popular works on child psychology and was encouraging teachers and mothers to work together to study the children in their care and share their observations with scholars. The introduction of the baby book—a blank book for recording developmental milestones, in addition to memories—dates to this era and impulse.[20] The "child study" movement was highly successful, engaging mothers in "securing accurate data for the use of scientists" such as those on the Committee on Child Study of the Society of Pedagogic Research (Normal College, New York City) and the New York State Department of Child Study. Topical "syllabi"—actually protocols for observation—were distributed to mothers so they could collect information on such issues as "children expressing 'choice,'" based on educational theory that "'in order to train citizens for a republic, children must early exercise the power of choosing.'"[21]

This increasing concern for boys coincided with the emergence of child psychology and its emphasis on the vital importance of the earliest experiences of infancy and childhood. It didn't matter that adults could not remember these experiences; if anything, the fact that these experiences were forgotten—or repressed—gave them even more power in shaping adolescent and adult lives, through unconscious fears and neuroses acquired in the womb, at the breast, or in the nursery.

> The first years of life, which the adult cannot remember, are fateful for health or disease, virtue or vice, success or failure. The younger the child is, the more he is the father of the man to be.[22]

This psychological view of the child conflicted with the sentimentalized Victorian view of the innocent, vulnerable child who needed to be shielded from adulthood. Both views are translated into distinct, conflicting beliefs about appropriate dress for boys, especially very little boys. Although most of the emerging psychological literature focused on adolescence, its strongest impact on clothing focused on that of infants and toddlers, from around 1900 to 1910. This timing coincided with the adulthood of boys born between 1880 and 1890 who wore or observed Fauntleroy suits at the height of their popularity.

Yet for all of these worries and all the pressure to mold a new breed of American boys, many parents still had a desire to protect children from the demands of adulthood, to prolong childhood, and to make it as sweet and pleasant as possible. This may seem contradictory, but then parents can be inconsistent! The father who gave his infant son cold baths to harden him against disease claimed in the same article never to have used corporal punishment. The clearest expression of this view of boyhood came from Dan Beard, founder of the Boy Scouts of America:

> The difference between the baldheaded, bearded boy and his younger brother in knickerbockers is that the latter is fond of fun and owns up to it, while the former is fond of fun and conceals the fact behind a solemn countenance and a severe and dignified frown.[23]

For many parents in the early 1900s, gender identity was tied uncomfortably closely to sexuality, which they believed did not fully emerge until adolescence, and even then should be subject to careful moral (parental) control. For these parents, infants and toddlers were asexual beings, and the only proper way to dress them was in clothing that concealed their sex. This was not only about adult perceptions of little children; according to this view, the children *themselves* should not be made aware of these differences until they were old enough to begin to understand them. Accordingly, gendered clothing should be acquired in stages, coinciding with the gradual emergence of masculinity and femininity and the child's grasp of those concepts, as understood in the context of recent findings in child psychology, which were spreading to advice literature and consumer culture.

Concerns about children's sexual development and gender identities were often at the center of this research and advice. This was particularly true of boys' sexuality, from concerns about masturbation to the origins of homosexuality. In the opinion of some psychologists at the time, boyhood masturbation opened the door to the entire range of "moral and physical degeneracy," including homosexuality.[24] The implications of this belief for boys' clothing were unclear, and the advice provided to mothers was consequently inconsistent. Some experts advocated pajamas instead of nightgowns as a preventative; others argued that bifurcated clothing, being fitted to the legs, was more likely to encourage masturbation than gowns. By that logic not only were pajamas off limits, but there also was an argument to be made against putting little boys in pants too early.

G. Stanley Hall believed that spontaneous nocturnal emissions (that is, "wet dreams") in older boys were "natural," but masturbation was a "scourge of the human race destructive of that perhaps most important thing in the world, the potency of good heredity." Perhaps more frightening to the already anxious parents of the era, he wrote that men who masturbated as teenagers would father children marked by "persistent infantilism or overripeness."[25] His fashion advice to mothers, published in the September 1907 issue of the *Ladies' Home Journal,* was that the child's first trousers should "bifurcate low down, be loose, not warm or rough, and pocketless," adding that "violation of any of these precepts before school age leads to self-consciousness, and predisposes toward temptation."[26]

Based on recent discoveries in human evolution and anthropology, Hall was also convinced that gender distinctions were a marker of advanced civilization. This led him to believe that equality between the sexes was unlikely in an advanced society because "with civilization the dimensions of the woman's body, her life, and her psychic traits become more different from those of men rather than less so." Evolution favored manly men and womanly women; racial survival was threatened by coeducation, women entering masculine professions, and male homosexuality.[27] Like many behavioral scientists influenced by the work of Sigmund Freud, Hall believed that homosexuality was the consequence of boys' inappropriate identification with their mothers and weak identification with their fathers. The solution was clear: since very young children were capable of learning gender identity (including the "wrong" one), sharp gender distinctions *should* be taught—and the earlier, the better. Boys needed to learn to be masculine in order to counter the apparent weakening of the sex under the pressures of the modern world and what seemed to be an alarmingly decadent culture, not to mention the legacy of their fathers' excessive masturbation! But how? And what role would clothing play in this transformation? Two new rules needed to be imposed on fashions for babies and small boys: existing markers of masculinity needed to occur earlier, and they needed to be sharper and more exclusive, so that even a child could grasp them.

Simply put, "modern," enlightened early twentieth-century parents came to believe that gender identity was the product of nurture and that gendered clothing should encourage its development, not signify its attainment, as had been the case for generations. For older boys, this meant earlier haircuts and trousers. But how do you make a baby or toddler look unambiguously masculine? There were three possible categories of visual cues to a child's sex that could have been applied: hair length, bifurcated clothes such as trousers, and stylistic clues such as fabric, decoration, cut, and color. The first (hair length) was dependent on the child's own available resources; a long-haired one- or two-year old could have his hair trimmed and parted like a boy's, but the bald-headed tot needed more by way of clues. The complex task of establishing which colors, motifs, and decoration were masculine and which were feminine took most of the twentieth century, as we'll see in the next chapter. That left the "pants are for boys" rule, somewhat complicated by the acceptance of rompers and creepers as neutral garments worn by girls and boys alike. The most obvious remaining option was lowering the age at which boys began to wear trousers instead of dresses or kilts, to the point of eliminating dresses from their wardrobes completely.

As late as the mid-1890s, fashion writers generally agreed that boys of two or three could wear kilts and blouses instead of one-piece dresses, but they discouraged mothers from putting boys in trousers until age five. At least that was what they wrote in their general articles; in the advice columns, where they responded to questions from individuals, they allowed more leeway. One mother wrote and described her four-year-old boy, giving his height and asking whether he should wear kilts or trousers. The answer was to dress the boy in short trousers, because he was as large as most boys at six years and would look awkward in skirts. Given parents' usual objectivity and the spread of the belief that boys would benefit from earlier identification with their fathers, the suggestion that large, "manly looking" boys could be put into trousers early undoubtedly helped fuel the trend away from dresses for preschoolers.

Around 1900, however, such an alteration may well have been fraught with conflict and confusion. In the first place, putting very little boys (under three years) in trousers collided with the belief that precocity in children was dangerous. Some authorities continued to lay out strict rules according to age. *Vogue* outlined the stages of boy dressing specifically: long dresses until six months, short dresses until age three, and then either Russian blouses with knickers or kilt suits up to the age of five or six. *Harper's Bazaar* noted that boys were usually put into trousers as soon as they were too old for baby frocks, at about three years. Despite this advice, toddler boys in photographs between 1900 and 1910 were

Boy in a Russian dress, around 1905. Russian tunics or dresses were distinguished by their stand-up collars and double-breasted styling.

University of Maryland Costume and Textile Collection

increasingly less likely to be wearing skirts and more likely to be wearing knickers or short pants. Some kilt suits even came with matching knickers, giving parents the choice to put their son in a kilt, trousers, or both. The extent of the contentiousness of this change is measurable in time: it took until the late 1920s before dresses were consistently limited to infants and girls, and they remained a small part of newborn layettes in part of the United States for another generation beyond that.

CLOTHING JUST FOR BOYS

It should be clear by now that distinguishing little boys from girls was not a simple matter of pink and blue. Even that story is complex enough to merit its own chapter. The changes in clothing styles for little boys over the course of the twentieth century reflected conflicting ideas about how masculinity is created and shaped. Another important factor was the contrast that sometimes existed between the symbolic "real" boy as he existed in literature and advertising and the actual boy in the nursery. Was the "real" boy the one who chafed at being cooped up and longed to run around outdoors, or was he the one in Althea Randolph's sentimental poem "A Secret":

> I love to play with dollies,
> I have one for a toy,
> I keep it very secret,—
> Because I am a boy![28]

1914

Even the experts agreed that not all boys were made of "snips and snails and puppy dog tails." G. Stanley Hall separated children into two classes, aggressive and passive, adding, "By no means do boys always belong to the aggressive class, and girls to the passive class."[29] Psychologist W. Ryman Boorman (1929) wrote sympathetically about a ten-year-old boy reacting tearfully to being mistaken for a girl. Boorman noted that "effeminacy is not uncommon among very young boys," and suggested that differentiating their clothing would help them avoid embarrassment.[30] Rather than keeping pace with boys' development or signifying new stages of life, clothing needed to take on a pedagogical or even therapeutic role. A little boy's apparel should set him clearly apart from girls and women, in order to coax him toward the emulation of older boys and men. "However much the mother may regret to part with curls and ruffles," an advice writer warned in 1916, "she should remember that the child's own sense of fitness is worthy of consideration; and she should help in the development of those qualities that later will make for manliness, by dressing him suitably now while he is a little boy."[31]

Certain details were considered essential for these lessons. A boy must have pockets; a girl could do without. Girls' dresses could button down the back, but boys' must open in front. For a baby's first short dress, gathers were for girls; vertical tucks or smocking should be used to control fullness in boys' dresses. Boys' pants must "be open in front, just like papa's." The same author provides a pattern for fly-front trousers and notes that, as was the case with rompers, clothing manufacturers were lagging behind their customers: "One objection to this is the impossibility of buying them so; but if mothers demand it, they will soon be in the market. Until that time, the fly can be adjusted to any pattern, and the trousers made by a seamstress."[32]

Regardless of how simple and straightforward these rules may seem, it is unlikely they were followed any more uniformly than most rules. Except for the use of fly closures on boys' pants, all of the other suggestions could just as likely have been adopted for girls—and they were, from time to time. Rather than depending on some feature that only boys' clothing would have, gender distinctions had to visually connect boys with men (by imitating men's styles as much as possible) and separate from girls' fashions by abandoning some elements altogether. This meant that little boys' clothing must be made plainer than it once had been. Boys "should not have to fuss over their clothes."[33]

> If you are going to sew for your son see to it that you do it well, not only for your own satisfaction but for his. Above all, never yield to the feminine instinct for frills and furbelows. Little Lord Fauntleroy went out of fashion long ago.[34]

The first "frills and furbelows" to go were lace, bows, ruffles, and other elaborate trims, not seen on toddler boys' clothing after the 1920s except for the very rare exception of the dressy button-on suit. Flowers (printed or embroidered) disappeared around the same time, and decorative motifs were reduced to transportation themes (boats, airplanes, cars), sports (balls, bats), male figures (cowboys, sailors, athletes), and selected animals (dogs, horses, bears), although some of these also appeared on girls' clothing, particularly in brother-sister outfits.

Boy, age three or four, in a button-on suit with a ruffled shirt.
Courtesy of the Maryland Historical Society.

It is essential to point out that many of these rules did not trickle down to infants' clothing for some time. Baby clothing manufacturers continued to offer a significant proportion of styles with no flowers and no airplanes until the 1980s, a phenomenon that will be discussed in greater detail in a later chapter. In addition, girls could wear many of the "tailored" styles marketed primarily to boys, since they were masculine only in their plainness. A striped T-shirt and shorts outfit, worn by a little girl in pigtails, would look tomboyish, a construct that remained acceptable for girls in a way that "sissy-ness" was not for boys.

The masculinization of fashions for boys under six attempted to solve one problem—perceived threats to white male dominance—but as often happens, the solutions created new social and cultural pressure points. First, by creating the "small boy consumer" as a creature with both needs and agency, the boys' clothing market moved Americans further down the road of consumption-based identity for children. As sociologist Daniel T. Cook has persuasively argued, the marketing of children's clothing to mothers as proxy consumers dates to this era. The identification of early boyhood as a stage where masculine behavior should be encouraged and offering masculine clothing as a response to a boy's needs, expressed and unexpressed, provided a clear mechanism for a mother's proxy consumption to shape her son's later consumption-defined identity. It also opened the door for fathers to be more involved in clothing decisions, once strictly a mother's prerogative. To a two-year-old child in 1880, being "a boy" was in some ways a matter of faith and aspiration, not fashion. By 1940, a two-year-old was able to identify himself—or another child—as a boy based on clothing alone. According to what we know today about children and gender, this suggests that children still pursuing gender permanence learned that clothing indeed "made the man." This capability would also have the effect of facilitating same-sex play, so important to social learning of gender. As long as boys of this age had a say in how they were dressed, they would be likely to prefer gender schematic clothing, and gendered clothing would grow in importance as each successive generation reached parenthood.

Second, replacing neutral clothing with gendered clothing for toddlers not only injected an awareness of difference but also invited children to connect those differences with sexual disparities in power, value, and opportunity, just when they were acquiring gender identity and wondering if gender was permanent. G. Stanley Hall, for all his conviction that men and women would never be equal in an advanced society, was disturbed by a U.S. Census study that showed that one-third of school-age girls wished they were boys. Seen in the light of German research that demonstrated the harm done by feelings of inferiority, Hall worried that girls' attainment of "womanliness" would be hampered by too much attention to boys in a way that suggested males were superior. He condemned the practice of punishing little boys by putting them back in dresses, noting that "to encourage children to believe boys are better than girls is to exert a vicious but very subtle influence."[35]

So the period that began with *Little Lord Fauntleroy* ended with boys' fashions rejecting every detail that might be construed as feminine. The mothers who amused themselves with "Guess the Baby's Sex" contests became the grandmothers who made old-fashioned baby dresses for a newborn's layette. And the little boys who had worn dresses grew up to be the fathers who said, "No, thanks" to grandmama's handiwork for their own sons.

PINK IS FOR BOYS

WHEN I FIRST ENCOUNTERED THE WORDS BELOW nearly thirty years ago, I stopped and reread them several times:

> Pink or Blue? Which is intended for boys and which for girls? This question comes from one of our readers this month, and the discussion may be of interest to others. There has been a great diversity of opinion on this subject, but the generally accepted rule is pink for the boy and blue for the girl. The reason is that pink, being a more decided and stronger color, is more suitable for the boy, while blue, which is more delicate and dainty, is prettier for the girl.[1]

I was following up a minor sideline in a small project on babies' clothing during the Progressive Era—the seemingly trivial question, "When were pink and blue introduced as gendered colors?" At that point, the white rabbit darted into its hole, and I dove in after it. Years later, I am back to tell the very complicated tale of how American baby and toddler clothing went from being completely devoid of sexual hints to almost completely separated into "his" and "hers" camps. And, for me, it all started with pink and blue.

Pink and blue symbolism is so firmly embedded in American popular culture that it's hard to believe that their gender associations are relatively new. As explained earlier, before 1900 most babies in the United States wore white clothing that signified their age but not their sex, consistent with cultural norms. Toddler and preschooler clothing (up to age six) was more colorful, but hues were assigned according to complexion, season, or fashion, not sex. Beginning in the early twentieth century, American children's fashions became progressively more gender-specific. The symbolism of pink, once considered one of many interchangeable pastel "nursery colors" with no gender associations, is a dramatic and visible marker of this change. While pink is often paired with blue in discussions of gender symbolism, blue has never been as powerful symbolically as pink. Girls can wear any shade of blue, as long as it is sufficiently modified with flowers, ruffles, and other feminine touches. But pink clothing for boys has grown increasingly rare since the 1940s.

The modern history of pink as a "girl's" color has three stages, with a fourth just emerging. The first stage paralleled the transition from un-gendered to gendered clothing for toddlers and children during the first half of the twentieth century, as details once considered "babyish" or youthful—including the color pink—were recast as "feminine," though this new rule was adopted slowly and inconsistently. From the late 1960s through the early 1980s, pastel clothing in general and pink in particular fell into disfavor, partly because of child development studies that indi-cated that babies found strong contrasts more interesting and partly as a result of the women's liberation movement, which associated the color pink with traditional female roles and notions of femininity. Since the mid-1980s, not only has pink become a strongly feminine color (prob-ably because the women's movement connected it with traditional girli-ness so successfully), but it has reached the level of moral imperative in the age group of three to seven. Finally, since around 2000, alternative and resistant uses of pink have appeared on the scene for both boys and girls. This uneasy, protracted transition traces the underlying shape of changing and conflicted attitudes toward sexuality as it is applied to in-fants and toddlers, in addition to uncertainty and anxiety about those parts of American culture identified as "feminine."

A BRIEF HISTORY OF PINK

"Pink" as a color name is a relatively recent addition to the English language; according to the *Oxford English Dictionary*, older meanings in-clude a young salmon, a kind of fishing boat shaped like a young salmon, a jagged fencing wound, and a method of decorating fabric by piercing or scalloping the edge—familiar to those of us who have used pinking shears to trim cloth. It's the latter meaning that probably gave rise to the popular name for a species of *Dianthus* (in the 1570s) and, based on the colors of that flower, the scarlet coats worn by foxhunters and the range of colors from a rosy lavender to soft corals. According to the *OED*, pink as a common name for a light or pale red dates only to the 1840s, although dye recipes for "pink" exist from the mid-eighteenth century.[2] The metaphorical use of these pastel shades of violet and red, as in "rosy-fingered Dawn," far predates their use as color names, of course, but the associations are evocative of a wide range of visual images, experiences, and characteristics—spring, health (as in "in the pink"), and youth—not of femininity. Young men and women might wear pink clothing; old men and women did not.

PINK AND BLUE AS AMBIGUOUS OR GENDER NEUTRAL COLORS

Up to the 1770s, colored dresses were common for infants, with dark red, yellow, and blue all being used. The introduction of bleaching and inexpensive cotton revolutionized nursery clothing and ushered in the era of the long white dress. For most of the nineteenth century, the dominant color for baby clothing was white. White baby clothing, which could withstand frequent laundering with boiling water, probably owed its long popularity in part to those practical considerations in addition to its connotation of purity and innocence.

Color was never completely absent from baby clothing and is often visible in portraits in the form of ribbons, sashes, or other elements that could be removed before laundering. Infants' and toddlers' white muslin or gauze frocks also featured colored underslips, sashes, and shoes. Pastel colors for these touches were quite popular, with pink, blue, and yellow the most common choices.[3] There is no evidence that pink and blue signified gender at all until the mid-nineteenth century, and even then, they did so inconsistently (sometimes pink was a boy's color, sometimes a girl's). A July 1856 news item in *Godey's Magazine and Lady's Book* about the preparations for the first child of Napoleon III and Empress Eugenie of France noted that the layette featured lots of white dresses with blue trim. This was because their firstborn would be a baby "*voué au blanc*" (dedicated to the Virgin) and would wear white and blue for its first seven years. This, the author explained, "symbolizes special protection," although in France blue was usually used for boys and rose for girls. This suggests that a girl dedicated to the Virgin would also wear only blue and white.

Advice and literary references were generally divided on the issue, as in these examples:

> Pure white is used for all babies. Blue is for girls and pink is for boys, when a color is wished. (*Ladies' Home Journal,* 1890)

"Amy put a blue ribbon on the boy and a pink on the girl, French fashion,
so you can always tell. Besides, one has blue eyes and one brown. Kiss them,
Uncle Teddy," said wicked Jo. (Louisa May Alcott, *Little Women*, 1880, 349)

More often, pink and blue were suggested as interchangeable, gender-
neutral "nursery colors," appearing together in many of the clothes and
furnishings found in the baby's room. An 1896 article in the *Delineator*
described bootees in white, blue and white, or pink and white, "infants'
colors all,"[4] and 1911 instructions for a layette (a newborn's wardrobe,
prepared before the birth) suggests white fabrics trimmed with "pale
pink, blue, or yellow."[5] Color options were subject to fashion as well.
Ladies' Home Journal writer Emma M. Hooper excluded pink from an
1893 list of fashionable shades for little girls' spring cloaks, suggesting
white, blue, tan, pearl gray, or brown instead.[6] A boy paper doll featured
in the September 1913 *Woman's Home Companion* was described as
disliking his new dress because it had "so many pink ribbons," until he
learned from the Paris lady doll that "pink ribbons were stylish, so he
didn't mind wearing his new dress. He even admired it."

The selection of pink or blue for an individual child at the turn of the
century could also be based on becomingness, according to nineteenth-
century rules of taste. Light shades were considered more flattering to the
pale complexions of Caucasian babies, and eye color was an important
factor in selecting the correct hue.[7] A portrait of twin infants (sex unknown) at the Strong Museum of Play probably illustrates the usual rule.
Both babies are wearing white dresses; the brunette twin wears pink booties; the blue-eyed blonde wears blue ones. The Winterthur Museum and
Library has a set of companion paper dolls that also follows this rule: one
doll, cut from a magazine, has brown hair, blue eyes, and blue trim on
her white undergarments. The original owner made a hand-drawn copy
with blonde hair, brown eyes, and pink trim. The few baby books that
included locks of hair or descriptions of hair or eye color also support
this pattern. Of the three locks of brown hair preserved in the books (two
boys and a girl), all were tied with pink ribbons. Four of the six blonde
locks (four girls and two boys) had blue ribbons (one of the boys and
three of the girls). The other blonde boy and girl both had pink ribbons.

Eventually, the old rules of "becomingness" were loosened and discarded. The creator of twin sister paper dolls, Madeleine and Gladys
(*Woman's Home Companion*, November 1920), provided this commen-
tary on their wardrobes:

Mad (brunette) wears yellow, blue, and green. Glad (blonde) wears green, purple, and pink. Some people think blondes ought not to wear pink, but that's because they don't know how becoming pink is to a really true blonde.

Evidence from fashion periodicals, vintage garments, paper dolls, and baby books is clear: boys under six wore pink clothing well into the twentieth century. In some cases it was combined with blue, or the child also had blue clothing in his wardrobe, indicating that it did not signify gender. A typical magazine or catalog description might read like this one from *Vogue,* February 22, 1900: "Everyday frocks for small boys, in either pale blue or pink." A 1920 set of brother-sister twin paper dolls in *Good Housekeeping* included a pink romper for one and a blue romper for the other and then switched the colors for a different outfit.

PINK AND BLUE AS GENDERED COLORS

In the 1880s, G. Stanley Hall published the first of his many scholarly and popular works on child psychology. By 1896, the influence of psychological studies was so widespread that a *Delineator* article on nursery decoration could base its recommendations on studies of infant development. As discussed in greater detail in the previous chapter, one of the changes advocated by child care experts after the turn of the century was greater and earlier distinction between girls' and boys' appearance. Since pink and blue were already sometimes used to signify gender, color coding might seem to be a likely candidate for this function. Unfortunately, the inconsistency of pink and blue symbolism prolonged the general acceptance of what is now considered the "traditional" pattern. One hundred twenty-one years separate the first reference to pink and blue as gendered colors (the 1856 *Godey's* article about Empress Eugenie's layette preparations) from the last example of pink clothes for boys that I could find (a baby brother paper doll with a pink snowsuit in 1977).

It is clear that pink-blue gender coding was known in the 1860s but was not dominant until the 1950s in most parts of the United States and not universal until a generation later. Why did it take so long? Not everyone was comfortable with the notion of accelerating gender identity, after generations of seeing babies as sexless cherubs. The changes in clothing reflected the inner ideal of emerging manliness—though not too much, or too soon, because that was also seen as dangerous. A more persuasive explanation is that the existing candidates for color symbolism—pink and blue, the popular nursery hues—had no consistent meaning, and sometimes contradictory meanings, in different cultures across post–Ellis Island America. Another factor was the continuing importance of homemade clothing for babies and small children. Although ready-to-wear clothing was increasingly popular, the younger the child the easier it was to sew its clothing, which allowed much more variation in color and fabric. This reduced the impact of decisions by manufacturers and retailers, even if they had been able to agree, which they hadn't, though not for lack of trying. In the 1918 *Infants' Department* article quoted at the beginning of this chapter, the anonymous author was discussing "the generally accepted rule" that pink is for boys and blue is for girls. He goes on to speculate on the reason for the confusion:

> The nursery rhyme of "Little Boy Blue" is responsible for the thought that blue is for boys. Stationers, too, reverse the colors, but as they sell only announcement cards and baby books, they cannot be considered authorities
>
> If a customer is too fussy on this subject, suggest that she blend the two colors, an effective and pretty custom which originated on the other side, and which after all is the only way of getting the laugh on the stork.

His indictment of the stationers seems unfair; baby announcements found tucked into baby books of that era (and as late as the 1960s) were more likely to be plain white or pink and blue together than one color or the other. The same was true of the baby books themselves, most of which were a solid color (brown leatherette was common) or pink *and* blue. Of the book covers that were pink or blue alone, there was still no clear gendered pattern. Of the eleven blue books, five belonged to girls and six to boys; out of twelve books with pink covers, seven were for boys and five for girls.

Surveys, catalog descriptions, and news articles dating from as late as the 1950s suggest that "a great diversity of opinion" continued to exist nationwide on the subject of pink and blue. Table 5.1 appeared in *Time* in 1927, based on surveys of infants' departments in major department stores:

There is a suggestion of a regional pattern; in Chicago—home to *Earnshaw's Infants' Department*—the largest department store agreed with the 1918 article that pink was for boys and blue for girls. This pattern predominated in midwestern and southern stores, but was reversed in New York, where much of the garment industry was located.[8] A Lord &

**Table 5.1. Color Preferences for Infants' Clothing in
Major U.S. Cities, 1927**

STORE	BOYS	GIRLS
Filene's (Boston)	Pink	Blue
Best's (Manhattan)	Pink	Blue
Macy's (Manhattan)	Blue	Pink
Franklin Simon (Manhattan)	Blue	Pink
Wanamaker's (Philadelphia)	Blue	Pink
Halle's (Cleveland)	Pink	Pink
Marshall Field's (Chicago)	Pink	Blue
Maison Blanche (New Orleans)	Pink	Blue
The White House (San Francisco)	Pink	Blue
Bullock's (Los Angeles)	Blue	Pink

Source: "Fashions: Baby's Clothes," *Time,* November 14, 1927.

Taylor survey of its New York area customers in 1937 revealed that about
three-quarters of them believed that pink was for girls and blue for boys,
and the rest preferred the reverse.

To further complicate the issue, baby clothes in other countries
were still following a variety of rules, meaning that imported items or
gifts from overseas continued to observe their own traditional patterns.
The 1927 *Time* article was inspired by news of the birth of a daughter
to Princess Astrid of Belgium, who had "optimistically" decorated the
cradle in pink, the traditional color for boys in that country. Blue was still
a "girl" color in Switzerland, and pink was an acceptable color for baby
boys in Korea in the 1980s.[9]

Lists of shower and birthday gifts appear occasionally in the baby
books in the UCLA collection, and these lend additional weight to my argument. Boys and girls alike received pink and blue gifts (clothing, blankets, and other items) all the way from the early 1900s through the early
1960s. Of the twenty-nine gift lists in girls' books, only nine contained
pink items but not blue ones; fourteen out of thirty-four boys received
only pink sweaters, booties, and other gifts. Exclusively blue gifts were

given to ten boys and six girls. A mixture of pink and blue gifts was most common for girls (fourteen) and as popular as blue items alone for boys (ten). Simply put, most babies born before 1960 were probably likely to receive pink gifts, regardless of their sex.

Birth announcements from the UCLA baby book collection tell a similar story. The earliest examples, from 1910 to 1920, are just small cards printed with the baby's name; when a color was used, it was limited to a narrow border, usually in pastel blue, whether for a boy or a girl. More colors, illustrations, and verses appear after 1920, but pink and blue were used together as "baby colors" well into the 1950s. Most did not mention the baby's sex, but just left a space for the child's name. Many baby books also include congratulatory baby cards received, valentines, and first birthday cards; of these only the latter were usually specifically designed for a boy or girl. Even these did not use pink and blue in the now traditional way, but repeat the patterns already noted for clothing: blue used when the child on the card is blue-eyed, pink used for both boys and girls, pink and blue used in combination as part of a "nursery" palette.

When did the modern gendered meanings of pink and blue become truly uniform and rigid? The Valentine Richmond History Center (Virginia) has in its collection a boy's pink linen short suit from the early 1960s.[10] There is anecdotal evidence that some German Catholics in Nebraska still preferred blue for girls and pink for boys in the 1960s, but no artifactual or photographic evidence. I have found baby brother paper dolls from 1963 and 1977 that have pink outfits. These examples are all clearly out of the mainstream. By the 1950s, pink was strongly associated with femininity. However, that connection was neither universal nor rigid; boys could still wear pink dress shirts and have pink frosting on their birthday cakes without risking gender confusion or public censure, and girls wore many colors besides pink.[11]

None of this transition happened by childcare expert fiat or industry proclamation. There was no sudden, unanimous cultural shift. It evolved over decades. At the same time, clothing manufacturers did their best to anticipate those choices better than their competitors and to shape those choices in order to make them more predictable and profitable. The more baby clothing could be designed for an individual child—and sex was the easiest and most obvious way to distinguish babies—the harder it would be for parents to hand down clothing from one child to the next, and the more clothing they would have to buy as their families grew. Pink and blue color coding might have been an ideal solution, clearly discernible (at least for 92 percent of the population with normal color vision) and easy to manufacture (just make up the same garments in two different colors). As it turned out, persuading people to follow a seemingly simple rule was complicated by taste, culture, and region. Probably for this reason, between 1900 and 1970 dozens of additional trims, decorative motifs, and garment details shifted slowly from the "baby" category to one side or the other of the gender binary divide, making boys and girls more easily identifiable first as toddlers and eventually as infants.

The effect of this clearer demarcation on children at a particular stage in the evolution of color coding can be determined indirectly by examining the way their own children were dressed through the lens of our current understanding of identity formation. According to modern gender identity theory, children learn what to call themselves—the words "boy" or "girl"—in infancy, then move on to the task of learning the complicated gender associations and expectations of those words, mostly by observation and interaction with peers and adults. Learning the broad outlines of gendered appearance and behavior takes until the child is around three, but most do not grasp that their own sex is permanent until they are five or six. In the meantime, how might they react to ambiguous or flexible gender symbolism or being mistaken for the "wrong" sex when dressed a certain way?

Consider the possibility that the very gradual gendering of pink and blue (and other garment details) was driven by the twin engines of young children's desire for sharper distinctions and an increasing inclination, by the grown-up children who were their parents, to satisfy that desire. The question then arises of why in the late 1960s there was a temporary suppression of gendered clothing and the trend of fifty or so years appeared to reverse.

PINK IN THE UNISEX ERA

The trend toward androgynous styles for teenagers and adults in the 1960s owed its popularity to a mixture of popular culture influences, but it had a serious subtext: a generational clash over old and new rules for sexual expression and behavior. By the late 1960s, traditional gender roles were themselves the object of scrutiny, bringing dress and appearance onto center stage. As baby boomers became parents, unisex clothing became even more of a philosophical and moral issue, as part of the larger trend known as nonsexist or gender-free child rearing.

The "unisex era" (1965–85) will be discussed in much greater detail in the next chapter, but the story of pink and its symbolism merits attention here. During the heyday of unisex child rearing in the 1970s, pink was so strongly associated with traditional femininity that it was vehemently rejected by feminist parents for their daughters' clothing.[12] At the height of the trend (the mid-1970s), Sears catalogs carried *no* pink clothing for toddlers and only a few pink items for babies. If nothing else, this rejection confirmed that pink had become an undeniable symbol of femininity. Another trend was shaping baby clothes: increased scientific study of infant development. For decades, infant clothing had been offered in pastels, while both pastels and dark colors had been popular for toddler clothing. As studies began to suggest that bright and contrasting colors were more visible and appealing to babies, pastels began to make way for the more saturated hues once reserved for older children. *Earnshaw's* reported in 1973 that, while solid pastels remained popular, other colors were becoming trendy (green, orange, yellow) as were plaids and stripes. Leading up to the 1976 bicentennial of the American Revolution, red, white, and blue were also popular.

In the mid-1970s, the objective of feminist parents was to empower girls by stripping their clothing of every last vestige of "traditional" femininity and replacing the ideal little lady of their childhood with the tomboy. There are tantalizing clues that, in removing pink and other "girly" elements from their daughters' clothing, the mothers of the 1970s (who were born in the late 1940s and early 1950s) were seeing the gendered clothing of their childhood through the lens of second-wave feminism. Julia Spiegel, owner of Makalu, a small children's wear design firm, added pink to her line in the mid-1980s when it began to regain its popularity. "Having grown up as tomboys," Spiegel and her partner had struggled to find a pink they "could live with."[13]

THE PINK GENERATION

Beginning around 1980, traditional femininity began to reappear in women's and girl's clothing, eventually transforming the appearance of even the youngest babies. As enthusiasm for unisex waned and then evaporated, neutral styles became harder to find. Boys' clothing became more boyish in style, color, and trim, and girls' fashions became girlier. Pastels regained their dominance of infants' clothing, with pink and light blue used consistently and universally in the finally "traditional" manner. Luvs introduced pink and blue disposable diapers in 1985, with slightly different padding for boys (in front) and girls (in the middle) so that there was a functional difference as well. (It is worth noting that this assumed difference works best on upright babies.)

Toddler fashions offered more neutral choices than infants' wear, although ungendered styles were harder to find than before. Some catalog retailers—Lands' End and Biobottoms, for example—carried wardrobe staples (turtlenecks and T-shirts, plain pants and shorts) in solid colors well into the mid-1990s. Pink was one of the options, but parents wishing to avoid it could certainly do so. Pink's very last gasp as a gender-neutral color occurred in the early 1990s with the popularity of neon colors—acid green, shocking pink, and brilliant turquoise—for fashions and accessories for all ages.

What forces lay behind the rapid rehabilitation of pink and its elevation as the most visible marker of femininity? Two possibilities seem plausible. First, the advent of prenatal testing, which could reveal the baby's sex, played an important role. Industry studies had long indicated that expectant mothers began to make clothing purchases in the second trimester. As long as the baby's sex was unknown until birth, those purchases were neutral by necessity; neutral options included white, pink, and blue mixed together and other pastel colors—maize, mint, lilac, and aqua. The more common prenatal testing became, the more likely it was that parents would be drawn to clothes that matched the only detail they knew about their baby—its sex. But what about the ideals of nonsexist child rearing? Wouldn't "liberated" parents still prefer neutral styles to pink or blue? The swift disappearance of neutral infant styles would suggest a complicated answer. Some feminist parents no doubt still preferred neutral baby clothing, but for the market to shift so dramatically suggests that (1) not all who followed the unisex trend had shared their enthusiasm for gender equality and unisex child rearing—sometimes what appears to be a philosophical choice is just fashion—and (2) some parents who endorsed Title IX and the possibility of girls growing up to be attorneys and doctors did not see pink clothing as a barrier to their daughters' future.

A third possibility is that little girls themselves, as consumers with considerable persuasive power, made their own preferences clear. Discussions of nonsexist child rearing nearly always included anecdotes about children rejecting their parents' efforts and insisting on traditional toys and clothing. One of the criticisms of second-wave feminism, especially unisex child rearing, was that it framed equality more in terms of girls "being like a boy" than boys being more effeminate. Everything "girly"—fashion dolls, play makeup, pink—was criticized and rejected. Some writers echoed G. Stanley Hall's warning published in 1915: "Whatever our views about the social or political status of the sexes, incalculable harm is done by fostering the idea of the superiority of the boy."[14]

Hall had been no champion of women's equality; he opposed co-education and any attempt to train women for traditionally male professions. But his understanding of early child development—and observation of little boys and girls—led him to theorize that punishing little boys by putting them back in their baby dresses created the belief in both boys and girls that being female was shameful and inferior. Parents and experts of the 1970s and 1980s wondered if denying girls the opportunity to express their femininity and pushing them to be more "like boys" might not be equally destructive. This concern was magnified when unisex efforts were actively resisted or rejected by their own children, as was the case with the "feminist failures" described by Carrie Carmichael in *Non-sexist Childraising* (1977), whose daughters clamored for Barbies and nail polish. Popular authors on children and sex roles, who had once been so sure of the possibility of nurturing a new generation of women by eliminating pink and other feminine markers, began to equivocate in the late 1970s. Much of this was based on their own experiences as parents and what appeared to be their failures at nonsexist child rearing. The girls were pushing back.

Jesse Ellison, born in 1978, recalled her unisex girlhood in an article for *Time:*

> As a toddler, they dressed me in overalls and cut my hair in an androgynous bowl cut. I didn't have Barbies; I had wooden blocks. Even my first name is evidence of their experiment in gender neutrality. You can't imagine how many times I've had to explain, "No, not Jessica, just Jesse. Like a boy."[15]

Just as the boys in Little Lord Fauntleroy suits grew up to be fathers who wanted their sons to look more masculine, the girls of the 1970s became women who wanted long hair, sexy underwear, and feminine dresses for themselves and gendered clothing and toys for their own offspring. I suspect that the little girls of the late 1960s and early 1970s may have been the driving force in reviving pink and blue color coding, assisted by the ability to know their child's sex months before birth. Ironically, the other force behind the crowning of pink as the principal signifier was probably the anti-pink crusaders of the 1970s themselves. By so openly and consistently associating pink with traditional femininity, they fixed it in public discourse as the most visible symbol of everything female.

WHY DO LITTLE GIRLS WANT PINK?

As unisex trends faded, pink became more and more the dominant color for girls under six, with its popularity peaking after 2000. Perhaps the most curious aspect of this fashion has been the apparent rejection of nurture and culture as the forces behind girls' preference for pink in favor of the conviction that girls are "wired" to favor that hue over others. This explanation was given the endorsement of science with the publication of several studies that "proved" that women preferred pink to blue.

The mostly widely cited study of this type appeared in *Current Biology* and was spread internationally by bloggers and news organizations.[16] Neuroscientists Anya Hurlbert and Yazhu Ling reported finding a "robust, cross-cultural sex difference in color preference," with the women in their sample preferring reddish-purple hues to those in the greenish-yellow region, while men showed a preference for colors in the greenish-yellow end of the spectrum. Despite the fact that their study used adults, not children, and did not specifically test their responses to "pink," their work morphed in the popular press into articles with titles such as "Why Girls Like Pink," "Girls Prefer Pink," and "At Last, Scientists Discover Why Blue Is for Boys but Girls Really Do Prefer Pink."

Almost immediately, critics appeared, taking exception to the leap of interpretation made by the popular press. Hurlbert and Ling, who have expressed surprise and dismay at the popular response, were kept busy doing interviews to clarify their research: explaining that the colors women preferred were not "pink" in the popular sense but colors that were closer to the red-purple end of the spectrum they were using, that men and women both preferred blue to other hues, that the findings were probably of greater interest to evolutionary biologists and neuroscientists than to clothing designers, and so on. In the meantime, articles touting pink goods from curling irons to laptops have referenced Hurlbert and Ling's research as part of their sales pitch.

RESISTING "PINKIFICATION"

There are signs of change in recent years, with the coming-of-age of the children of the mid-1980s. The evidence is emerging from many directions. Playful reinterpretations of "traditional" feminine styling such as punk baby girl outfits in pink and black and other colors—purple, turquoise, green—are sharing rack space with more conservative styles. Even more telling, older boys and men are reclaiming pink. Pink dress shirts and ties have enjoyed a revival, beginning around 2004.[17] My son's college Ultimate team's colors are pink and black; until they actually ordered team uniforms in 2008, they wore women's pink T-shirts, hoodies, and warm-up pants found in thrift stores. Hearing about this book, a colleague passed along her son's favorite T-shirt from third grade, purchased at a local J. C. Penney store—a light pink shirt with these words:

> **10** REASONS I WEAR PINK
> It was my last clean shirt.
> My Mom made me wear it.
> I make this color look good.
> My Dad did the laundry.
> I wear this shirt to annoy you.
> Smart people wear pink.
> It's my party shirt.
> Pink is the new black.
> It's a fashion statement.
> And last but not least,
> TOUGH GUYS WEAR PINK!

Because pink and blue are so often named together, it is easy to see them as equivalents. But they are not. They don't carry the same weight or wield the same symbolic power. Baby girls can wear blue, as long as other style elements—ruffles, puffed sleeves—override the weak "masculine" significance. But pink trumps any and all attempts to neuter it. When my son and his teammates wear pink, it's a humorous act that depends on the contrast between the feminine color and their own masculinity. Whether used traditionally, humorously, or ironically, pink is still a symbol of femininity and likely to remain so for some time.

UNISEX CHILD REARING AND GENDER-FREE FASHION

THE HISTORY OF THE LAST 125 YEARS in American children's clothing is a tale of progressively and increasingly genderized fashions, particularly for babies and toddlers. Since the 1880s, pink and blue color coding has replaced traditional white infant clothing, and pants have supplanted dresses for toddler boys. Ungendered fashions—either designed for both boys and girls, or boys' styles acceptable for girls' play clothes—played an increasingly small but still important role in children's wardrobes in the twentieth century. Then came the mid-1960s, when gender-bending or androgynous fashion took center stage under the label "unisex."[1] Flourishing for about twenty years, unisex clothing stands out as a significant pause in the overall trend toward more gendered children's clothing. Between 1965 and 1985, boys sported long hair and wore boldly patterned shirts and pants; girls wore pants, even for school. Sears, Roebuck & Co. carried no toddler clothing in pink from 1976 to 1978. For a while, it appeared that gendered clothing was a thing of the past and that children were, in the words of a popular song, "Free to Be You and Me." But as swiftly as it had appeared, the unisex trend faded. Neutral styles for infants were reduced to a very small part of the market in the mid-1980s, and by the mid-1990s styles for toddlers and young children were more gender specific than they had been in the 1950s. In this chapter, I suggest that understanding unisex clothing requires us to consider this brief but significant period not only in opposition to gendered clothing but also as part of the longer story of neutral fashions. It is also an opportunity to examine children's clothing trends through a developmental lens and from a generational perspective.

The women's liberation movement and the sexual revolution of the 1960s and ensuing arguments over gender and appearance (particularly the appropriateness of pants for women and long hair for men) height-ened public awareness of how "costume" reflects the roles we play. In the early 1970s, the discussion expanded to include children, with the con-cept of nonsexist child rearing encouraging many parents to dress their children more androgynously. In the decades leading up to unisex design, the definition of "neutral" had been shifting almost imperceptibly, be-coming a smaller and smaller list of features and colors; details such as lace and flower motifs once acceptable for either sex had gradually been recategorized as feminine. Despite this rethinking of once-neutral ele-ments into more gendered details that would mark clothing as "for a boy" and "for a girl," neutral clothing articles still were important parts of the wardrobe, especially for babies and children under six. Hand-me-downs were common in large families, with parents reusing many items for chil-dren of either sex. In some cases, these pass-down items were expensive garments—tailored coats and snowsuits—worn infrequently enough to be presentable even after several owners. Baby clothes, especially in the smallest sizes, were also ideal candidates for reuse, since infants grow so fast in the first year.

Beyond these practical explanations, parental choice (seen in the baby record books) and advertisements for clothing items strongly sug-gest that popular ideas about gender and small children were much more flexible in the 1950s than we see in today's children's clothing depart-ments. Not only was there a higher comfort level with ambiguity, as evi-denced by the persistence of neutral clothing, but parents were comfort-able with boys wearing clothing featuring fabrics, colors, and decorative motifs that today would be considered feminine. For example, dainty embroidered batiste infant dresses, which had been traditional for new-borns for a century, were still included in boxed layette sets—intended for either sex—in the 1958 Sears catalog.

Neutral clothing options in the 1960s were not limited to the lay-ette or closets of schoolchildren; adult fashions began to be less rigidly gendered as well. After 1962, an increasing number of designers offered menswear looks for women, including the pantsuit. Floral prints, ruffles, and other "feminine" details for men were widely available, as were new looks intended for either, such as turtleneck shirts, caftans, and ponchos. Beneath the apparent playfulness of these "unisex" styles, an attempt to reform the status quo was emerging. These challenges were serious and sometimes controversial. School and work dress codes were written to prohibit long hair on boys and men or pants on women, some even leading to battles in court. Eventually fashion won out and unisex styles prevailed.

The most significant change for girls and women was the wider acceptance of pants. First-wave feminists had challenged men's exclusive right to trousers in the nineteenth century. By the early 1960s, trousers in many forms—jeans, capris, shorts, and pajamas—were acceptable leisure styles for American women, particularly the young. Unisex styles promised—or threatened, depending on one's point of view—to push this acceptance past existing boundaries once more and this time, even further. Dressier styles and trouser suits in menswear fabrics appeared, even as possible career wear options for women. This shift included a clothing construction detail that must seem charmingly harmless to young women today, but it sent a shudder through my middle school home economic teacher's large frame when she lectured about this detail in 1963: zippers installed in the center front, or fly, rather than in the side or back. The side or back zipper placement was considered more ladylike. "Women don't *need* front flies," she declared, as we bit our tongues to refrain from pointing out the even greater absurdity of side zippers.

By the late 1960s, women were agitating for wider acceptance for trousers, particularly in school and work settings. Some of these arguments grew out of second-wave feminism and the women's movement, but there were practical reasons for replacing pants with skirts. Miniskirts, another 1960s fashion trend, had become so short that any claims that skirts were more "modest" than pants for women were patently ludicrous. Some fashion writers at the time declared the death of the dress, as women of all ages adopted pants for a wider range of occasions.

FEMINISM AND NONSEXIST CHILD REARING

The trend toward unisex styles for teenagers and adults in the 1960s owed its popularity to a mixture of popular culture influences, but its serious subtext is indebted to two linked forces: feminism and the generational clash over old and new rules for sexual expression and behavior. Pants for women and long hair for men were far more than lighthearted fashion trends; they were the visible battle lines in the first skirmishes of today's culture wars.

Let's look at the generational push toward gender-free fashion. Admittedly, most teenagers in the 1960s did not have culture war in mind when they emulated their musical idols or adopted the fresh designs of London's Carnaby Street. Like generations of young people before them, young adults tried to express themselves and look attractive; like generations of parents before them, their mothers and fathers objected to styles they perceived as silly, wasteful, or immodest. However perennial this generational pattern of experimentation and testing had been, the 1960s were different, thanks to the sheer size of the baby boom population and the social and sexual upheavals that accompanied their coming of age.

For young men, clothing choices in the 1960s and 1970s included styles that challenged existing gender norms, ranging from Romantic revival (velvet jackets and flowing shirts) to a pastiche of styles borrowed from Africa and Asia. This "peacock revolution"—a reminder that men, like some bird species, could be fully feathered and preened—promised to restore the lost glory of flamboyant menswear. Once the rule in European costume, expanded color palettes and a profusion of decorative details represented a very direct challenge to the conformity and drabness of menswear at midcentury. For men and boys, perhaps the most contentious and visible aspect of unisex fashion concerned not clothing but hair. The British Invasion in popular music deserves much of the credit for the trend toward longer hair for men, thanks to the mop head silhouette of the Beatles and other groups. (However, the early photos of John Kennedy Jr.—born 1960—remind us that long bangs for little boys were an established look, particularly among upper-class Americans in the Northeast.) Just as trousers for women had been a point of contention for decades, long hair for men marked a significant cultural battle line for most of the 1960s and the early 1970s. Women also experimented with cut and length. In 1967, British fashion model Twiggy popularized a close-cropped "boy" haircut for women, and the stage was set for several years of gender-bending confusion about hairstyles.

Unisex clothing and hair trends for teens, young adults, and adults echoed in children's clothing, though to a lesser extent for infants than for toddlers. Nehru jackets enjoyed a brief fad in 1967–68 for boys right down to infancy, bringing with them turtleneck shirts and sweaters, which remained a durable neutral staple for years.[2] This imitation effect where adult trends were copied in miniature for children was not the only pressure for gender-free clothing. As noted in chapter 5, bright colors

BOYS' JACKET, OVERALLS AND SHIRT

Boys' jacket, overalls, and Nehru-collared shirt with ruffle, 1968. Note the "Beatles" haircuts.

Courtesy of The McCall Pattern Company copyright © 2011.

were replacing traditional pastels for babies and toddlers, due in part to studies suggesting that babies preferred them and in part to a rejection of pink and blue color-coding. *Earnshaw's Infants, Girls and Boys Wear Review* explained the difference only in terms of taste and practicality: some mothers preferred pastels for toddlers as more "babyish," as a positive signal about age, while more practical moms preferred dark colors that hid dirt and stains better.[3]

BABY X IN FICTION AND FACT: "ARE SEX ROLES NECESSARY?"

The sexual revolution and the women's liberation movement added a heightened element of rebellion to what might have otherwise been a more routine intergenerational conflict over skirt lengths and clothing fads. The popularity of unisex styles helped focus public attention on the relationship between gender and appearance, especially among young adult consumers. As the baby boomers became parents and began to make clothing decisions for their own children, unisex clothing became even more of a trend. A stream of popular culture, from adult fashions to children's books and music, broadcast the new ideal of unisex child rearing. In the early seventies, this idea of nonsexist child rearing encouraged many parents to dress their children more androgynously.

A pivotal event in this saga occurred in 1972, when *Ms.* magazine published a futuristic short story by Lois Gould entitled "X: A Fabulous Child's Story," in which a child's life was described with no reference or clues to gender. This fictional child brought to the surface many of the underlying questions about the cultural, social, and biological origins of gender roles. Were femininity and masculinity innate or learned? What was more powerful: nature or nurture? "X: A Fabulous Child's Story" framed and accelerated the "nature or nurture" debate in a manner that provoked discussion in living rooms and conference rooms for at least a decade. Evidence of this discussion can be found both in popular magazines (*Newsweek, Psychology Today*) and in professional journals (particularly *Sex Roles*, launched in 1975), but especially in women's magazines, including *Ms., Redbook, Essence, and McCall's.* The article titles alone speak volumes about parents' concerns and the ideological bent of the authors:

"Androgyny vs. the Tight Little Lives of Fluffy Women and Chesty Men"
(*Psychology Today,* September 1975)

"Does a Boy Have the Right to Be Effeminate?" (*Psychology Today,* April
1979)

"Do Children Need Sex Roles?" (*Newsweek,* June 10, 1974)

The *Ms.* "X" story also provided a model for scores of real-life studies that
explored the relationship between a child's sex (real or assumed) and the
child's interactions with adults. The earliest published study was Seavy
et al.'s 1975 "Baby X: The Effect of Gender Labels on Adult Responses
to Infants." In the study, a female infant, dressed in a yellow jumpsuit,
was presented to adult subjects with instructions to play with the baby.
Three toys were provided: a football, a rag doll, and a flexible plastic ring.
The baby was not named, which seemed stressful to the adult subjects.
(If asked, the experimenter expressed uncertainty regarding which baby
was in the study that day.) Later studies made the baby's perceived sex
the variable, for example, the same baby dressed in pink and named Beth
and dressed in blue and named Adam, with three toys (duck, doll, train).[4]
Other studies focused on how well children learned these stereotyped
clues or how adults' use of these clues may or may not reveal their own
beliefs about sex, gender, and appropriate behavior.

Multiple studies between 1975 and the mid-1980s established that
children understand and can apply gender stereotypes well before they
reach their third birthday. These studies also demonstrated that adults
routinely look for and use gender clues in their social interactions with
babies and toddlers. These "Baby X" studies only served to intensify
the fear that this "gendering" was harmful to children, especially girls.
Feminist thought in the late 1960s and 1970s cast traditional women's
clothing as villainous—limiting, objectifying, and disempowering. At
that time, from that perspective, many saw a direct correlation between
the trappings of femininity—sexy underwear, high heels, frilly dresses—
and women's reduced expectations and prospects. Likewise, many perceived a clear association between men's clothing—especially pants—
and empowerment.

Perhaps nothing captures the earnest revolutionary flavor of feminist approaches to child rearing as well as *Free to Be You and Me,* the criti-
cally acclaimed and highly popular album, book, and television special.

The *Free to Be You and Me* trio of media forms resulted from a collaboration between actress Marlo Thomas and Letty Cottin Pogrebin. They were, arguably, two of the era's more persistent and eloquent advocates for nonsexist child rearing. Their mutual friend Gloria Steinem made the creative match just as the Ms. Foundation for Women was being formed. Pogrebin recalls the beginning conversation:

> We all agreed that we wanted to help children to be unencumbered by stereotypes—to capitalize on their unique strengths and understand that whatever their gender, race, or ethnic identity, or their economic origins, they were free to pursue their talents and their dreams. *Free to Be* had to say all of this—and it had to be fun and entertaining, too![5]

The album, released in 1972, won a Grammy nomination. The 1974 TV special won both an Emmy and a Peabody Award, and it continues to be available on videotape, DVD, and now in YouTube clips. The book *Free to Be You and Me* has stayed in print since its publication in 1973.[6]

The recurring "two babies" sketch in *Free to Be You and Me* features the voices of Mel Brooks and Marlo Thomas animating a pair of newborns who are not sure what sex they are but attempt to guess, based on the stereotypes they have already learned. Since both are dressed in long white gowns, they rely on Brooks's "dainty feet" and Thomas's bald head. They decide, based on that evidence, that Brooks is a girl and Thomas a boy—until Thomas points out that Brooks is also bald. Finally, the matter is settled at diaper-changing time. This sketch essentially translates the "X" story into a humorous tale for children—and their parents—about the rather arbitrary nature of gender conventions and stereotypes.

Moving toward gender-free choices for boys and men raised a rather disturbing subtext in the broad cultural discussion. A strong element of homophobia in the public conversation about unisex clothing for both men and boys argued for restraint in redefining masculinity of their clothing. Even before the introduction of unisex child rearing, some critics questioned whether "liberated" men and women would make good gender role models for their children. Writing in 1970, journalist Barbara Wyden found the idea of longhaired daddies in beads and shorthaired mommies in pants disturbing enough to suggest that adult unisex fashion choices were "a symptom that their family needs help."[7] Negative reactions to the flourishes and expressiveness of the peacock revolution were nearly always couched in homophobic terms.

Tomboyism and women's appropriation of menswear, on the other hand, was seen not only as much less threatening but also as appealing and even sexually attractive. Given this cultural tilt, observers should not be surprised that unisex clothing ultimately meant that pants, even for school and dressy occasions, became an acceptable option for girls and women. Popular acceptance of pants for girls certainly echoed what was happening in fashion for women; *Earnshaw's* Marshall Gibralter explained the decline in dress sales for girls by noting, "Once the mother bought many dresses and an occasional pair of pants [for herself]. Now that is reversed." He connected the trend to more casual lifestyles, not to contested gender roles, which he did not even mention. If mothers—especially women in their early twenties—were wearing pants instead of skirts, this choice had nothing to do with gendered social trends.[8] This line of reasoning was prevalent in *Earnshaw's*, which tended to avoid taking sides in the culture wars over sexual expression and ascribed fashion trends to other, less controversial factors. More casual lifestyles were certainly influential, but informality alone would not have had an impact on what defined acceptable masculine and feminine dress. The changes that parents were demanding in children's clothing had less to do with lifestyle and more to do with ideas about gender identity formation.

UNISEX AND THE CHILDREN'S CLOTHING MARKET

The structure of the children's clothing market is significant in understanding the reach of unisex clothing. Large-scale manufacturing and merchandising had long been characteristic of the industry, with a few giant manufacturers such as Baby Togs, Carter's, and Health-Tex reaching consumers through local department stores or national chains. A significant proportion of children's clothing was manufactured by and sold through large catalog-based companies for most of the twentieth century. At the high end of the economic scale were companies that sold their products through more exclusive department and specialty stores. Until the mid-1980s, the retail giants in children's wear were Sears, Roebuck & Co., Montgomery Ward, and J. C. Penney, who together accounted for a quarter of the infant and toddler market.[9] Their print catalogs offer insight into the shape of the unisex trend, both in the variety of offerings and their location in the "big book." For example, the Spring 1970 Sears catalog featured "his and hers" styles for adults, displayed on the same page; these options included "family styles," modeled by school-age children. In the children's section, many similar styles for boys and girls were available, but these choices were displayed in the appropriate sections by age and sex, not on the same page. Only toddler unisex styles were shown together: overalls, pants, and shirts in blue, red, and green. Other, more traditional gender-specific styles were listed under "boys" and "girls."

The Fall 1970 Sears catalog asked, "What's fashion news and such fun to wear? Clothes both boys and girls can wear." These flexible styles were offered in sizes 2–6 (boys) and 2–6X (girls). Styles for older children and teens reflected the same gender-bending trends, but did not promote their similarity. For example, boys' clothing featured more patterns and brighter colors, while offerings for girls included many more trousers, but each set of choices occupied the appropriate pages by department for that sex.

Still, unisex in the 1970s Sears catalogs definitely meant "masculine clothing for women and girls," not vice versa. For example, boy-to-girl size conversion tables appeared in the teenage boy sections of the catalog from 1970 to 1980, clear acknowledgment that teenage girls were buying boys' clothing. In an interesting use of space in the catalog, similar (or even identical) styles were sometimes located in both the boys' and girls' sections. For example, plain turtleneck shirts and corduroy overalls in primary colors could be found in both departments. Cut and fabric were not the only genderless characteristics of these clothes. Compared with both previous and modern styles, children's clothing of the 1970s and early 1980s featured fewer pastels in favor of brighter and more saturated colors. One color in particular took a hit; there was much less pink, especially for babies and toddlers. This was true even when a garment was styled for a girl, as with the toddler shortall (short overall) and overall sets with ruffled straps and puffed-sleeve shirts in the Spring 1978 Sears catalog, available in red, yellow, or green but not in pink. Other pastels were more available: three-packs of undershirts for babies and toddlers came in a choice of all white or one each in pastel blue, yellow, and aqua.

Unisex clothing and fashion for boys meant a kind of flexibility that had not been seen in several decades: longer hair and more variety in fabrics, including floral prints, brighter colors, and more embellishment, especially embroidery. These trends slightly rolled back the stylistic changes that had been negotiated by the parents of the 1940s and 1950s, that is, by the parents of feminist parents. This openness for boys, however, did not reverse all of the earliest stylistic changes—baby boys did not begin wearing dresses again.

Among these "refreshed" or recycled choices, some significant styles worn by both boys and girls were truly unisex, in that these choices had no strong, preexisting gender significance. For example, new hairstyles emerged for boys and girls—and their parents: the shag (better known today as the mullet), serf (a 360-degree page boy), and the Afro. Fashion choices without a previous gendered incarnation included ponchos, vests, and turtleneck shirts. Similarly novel details embellished clothing, including large-scale prints, brightly colored fabrics, and giant zippers. Casual styles such as T-shirts, sweatshirts, sweatpants, and jeans, which had been ungendered for some time, became more popular for both sexes and permissible for a wider variety of occasions.

One of the most striking—and ironic—effects of the unisex clothing era is that pink finally became an unambiguously feminine color. Let's review the evolution and ossification of this gendered color. Although pink had been used fairly consistently as a girls' color ever since the end of World War II, particularly in the United States, examples persist of this color used either in neutral clothing or for boys well into the 1960s and 1970s. (Admittedly, by the 1970s, the number of pink items as neutral or boy options was extremely limited.) Pastel neutral styles for toddlers were replaced with brighter, more saturated, or darker hues: red, navy blue, green, orange, yellow, and brown. This trend was also quite noticeable in girls' styles in the same size range, with items offered in navy, brown, or red but not in pink. Not until 1978 did pink clothing for toddler girls reappear in the pages of Sears catalogs. Small wonder that anyone old enough to remember the mid-1970s finds the recent "pinkification" of girls' environment astonishing.

WHAT SHOULD JENNIFER AND JOSH WEAR?

While the battle between nature and nurture raged in the popular media throughout the 1970s, parents were left to clothe and raise their children with no clear agreement and with confusing advice from the "experts." The only common theme in the advice literature was the assertion that the stakes were very high: whether gender was a consequence of nature or nurture, children's future mental health and happiness were at stake. People on both sides of the controversy seemed to agree on the

Unisex toddler fashions, 1970.

Courtesy of Simplicity Creative Group.

tremendous power of the gender-shaping abilities of clothing. Feminist writers argued that traditional gendered clothing would make children repressed, rebellious, and unable to function in the new egalitarian society. More conservative voices warned that blurring the distinction between the sexes would produce an entire generation of homosexuals.[10] By the early 1980s, even the proponents of nonsexist child rearing were starting to take on an equivocating tone, emphasizing the murky areas and contradictory studies instead of offering parents clear guidance.

And of course, in the meantime, the children of the unisex era grew up and became parents, and they had their own views on the issue. Some people I talk to have connected the regendering of clothing to Reagan era conservatism. However, the likely truth is that the correlation may be possible, but there is no evidence of direct causation. The defeat of the Equal Rights Amendment and the rejection of unisex clothing occurred at roughly the same time and probably stemmed from the same conservative impulses, but that is too simple an explanation. Those impulses might be read, to a limited extent, in the clothing of babies and toddlers during the 1980s, in the pages of child-rearing books and articles, and in the ultimate rejection of unisex styles by the children who initially wore them.

One possible explanation for this shift is demographics. Between 1980 and 1990, the proportion of births to first-time parents shifted from baby boomers and generation Xers, with the crossover occurring in the late 1980s, shown in table 6.1. This fine-grained generational analysis matters because of the huge difference between being a twenty-three-year-old choosing gender-bending clothing for yourself in 1975 and having unisex clothing selected *for* you as a three-year-old. Just as the boys in velvet cavalier suits (circa 1890) grew up to be the fathers (circa 1910) who wanted their sons to look masculine, this suggests that the children of the 1970s became parents likely to prefer gendered clothing for their own offspring.

ALTERNATIVES AND RESISTANCE TO UNISEX

Not everyone follows fashion trends; in fact, many people actively resist trends while being perfectly aware of them. *Free to Be You and Me* won awards and sold millions of records, books, and videotapes,

Table 6.1. Age of First-Time Parents in 1975, 1980, 1985, and 1990 by Birth Cohort

	BIRTH COHORT	AGE IN 1975	% 1980 births	% 1985 births	% 1990 births
Mother	1961–75	0–14	<1	43	**71**
	1946–60	15–29	**79**	**56**	29
Father	1961–75	0–14	0	24	**53**
	1946–60	15–29	**82**	**71**	47

Source: U.S. Census Bureau, "1951–1994 Statistical Abstracts."

but that did not mean its message won universal approval. A parent who read *Psychology Today, Ms., Parents' Magazine, McCall's,* or *Good Housekeeping*—or who even talked to other parents—would probably be familiar with the arguments for nonsexist child rearing and unisex clothing, but not necessarily persuaded by them. Conservative parents generally rejected unisex child rearing along with other elements of feminist ideology, while less ideologically driven parents simply found gender-free clothing less appealing. Both classes of parents certainly had access to clothing choices other than gender-free throughout the era. Sears might not offer pastel toddler clothing, but specialty stores did, and in the 1970s many women still knew how to sew, which gave them many more options. And popular culture is complex and often contradictory; at the same time that girls were being encouraged to wear simple, modern styles, the television series *Little House on the Prairie* (1974–82) was popularizing romanticized versions of nineteenth-century girls' dresses.

Even as unisex fashions were enjoying wide popularity among adults, observers and industry insiders could see indications that the allure of traditional femininity was not forgotten. Diane Von Furstenberg's jersey wrap dress (1973) lured many women away from pants, and the disco craze reintroduced not only "touch" dancing but also clingy, feminine dresses. The founding of Victoria's Secret in 1977 was yet another sign that unisex clothing was not the only outlet for expressing women's new freedoms and identity expressions.

EXIT UNISEX; ENTER PINKIFICATION

As enthusiasm for unisex fashions waned and then evaporated in the early 1980s, children's clothing did not simply reset to earlier patterns of cut and color; neutral styles dwindled dramatically between 1984 and 1986. Boys' clothing design pushed toward greater masculine symbolism, extending the distance between boys and girls. A red T-shirt was not enough; the front needed an airplane or football appliqué. Girls clothing, on the other hand, retained the most revolutionary change that had occurred: pants remained wardrobe staples even for school and dressy occasions. However, pants—and every other clothing item for girls—began to acquire more and more feminine details and styling. In the vernacular, these clothing items became girlier—girlier than any previous generation, in fact. Hospitals reported a sharp increase in the frequency of ear piercing for baby girls; headbands and baby barrettes appeared in stores, and Luvs introduced pink and blue disposable diapers. Infant clothing departments—across a cross section of market targets from modest to designer—offered more gender-specific styles and fewer neutral options.

Between 1980 and 1990, the proportion of births to first-time parents shifted from baby boomers to generation Xers, with the crossover occurring around 1985–87. That boy who wore Garanimals separates—a staple unisex brand of the 1970s—now cradled his own child. If a boy, that infant was more likely to sport an NFL logo or "Little Slugger" graphic than had his father. The 1970s girl who wore a blue denim OshKosh B'gosh skirted overall over a cardinal red turtleneck and tights grew up to be the mother dressing her daughter to the nines with a ribbon and eyelet headband and lavender "onesie" with pink embroidery.

From the early 1970s to the mid-1980s, feminist child-rearing philosophies and a popular conversation about gender roles had resulted in a brief reversal of the gradual trend toward more gender-specific clothing, begun a century earlier. Beginning in the late 1970s, infants' clothing departments offered more gender-specific styles in addition to the unisex options. It would appear that parents in the younger cohort—those who were little boys and girls in the late 1960s and early 1970s—may have been the driving force in accelerating this trend in the mid-1980s. Perhaps the most intriguing feature of this change is that, in contrast to the masculinization of boys' clothing in the early twentieth century, the earliest and swiftest alteration to unisex fashion was the reintroduction of stereotypically feminine styles.

Hats and bonnets for babies are old news, but hair ribbons and barrettes for infants are a very recent innovation. These accessories took the industry by storm in 1988, signaling the end of unisex in infants' clothing. In 1978, the objective was to empower girls by eliminating every last vestige of "traditional" femininity from their environment. Just ten years later, traditional feminine styling was rebounding in girls' clothing, transforming the appearance of even the youngest babies. Pink, surely, would signal that the wee one in the stroller was a girl. Parents who dressed their daughters in primary colors or pastels other than pink were annoyed by the repeated cases of mistaken identity. However, the strong signal of pink was still lost on some of the older generation. Bear in mind that even in the mid-1980s it was possible to encounter elderly people who did not necessarily see pink as a gendered color. Add to that number the 7 percent of the male population with some form of red-green color blindness, and it is clear that pink alone was not always sufficient to communicate gender at the level of clarity desired by post-unisex parents.[11]

When adult fashions change suddenly—as in this decisive move toward pink for girls—the most reasonable explanations lie in other recent trends and events. Unraveling the motivations behind changes in children's fashions, however, is more complicated because the younger the child, the less agency she enjoys or exercises. Adults—mainly parents and grandparents—purchase infants' and toddlers' clothing. These adults are reacting not only to their own contemporary contexts but also to past contexts: their own memories of childhood. This creates an echo in young children's clothing that requires us to look back twenty years to explain dramatic changes and to look ahead twenty years to understand its impact.

Children's unisex clothing, which peaked in popularity in the 1970s, is one such moment. Although at first glance this pattern would seem to be an anomalous blip in the steady transition from ungendered to gendered children's clothing, unisex clothing provides a view both back to the postwar childhoods of the baby boomers and forward to the complex, gendered culturescape of the twenty-first century.

The 1970s were the place where the idealism of the 1960s met real life. The intersection was an interesting mix of experimentation, nostalgia, social engineering, and trial and error. My exploration of nonsexist child rearing and its relationship to unisex clothing trends of the period makes me somewhat reluctant to overgeneralize about parents and children of this time period. After all, this gender-free clothing impulse was just one style out of many, in a decade devoted to individualism. But it seems safe to say that unisex clothing options represented a controversial issue about which thoughtful parents could not help but be aware, even if they chose to disagree. What adults—parents and historians alike—tend to forget is that children, with their big ears and even bigger eyes, soaked up this controversy.

GENDERED AND NEUTRAL
CLOTHING SINCE 1985

IN THE GENERATION SINCE THE END of the unisex child rearing experiment, infants' and toddlers' clothing has changed from a market where neutral options were plentiful and even gendered clothing came in a wide range of colors to a consumerscape that is largely gender binary. So narrow are the choices that parents who wish to avoid gender stereotypes cannot shop in most mass-market retailers, whose neutral offerings are limited to newborn sizes. This shift occurred rapidly, beginning with the transformation in baby clothing around 1985. Suddenly, overalls, pants, and knitted tops, once staple neutral wardrobe items, were embellished with flowers or trucks. The infants' departments in large stores were more sharply divided into "boys" and "girls" sections, with less space devoted to neutral styles.

The continued influence of parental anxiety about gender and sexuality is no doubt a factor in this change, since there is no evidence that it had ever disappeared. If anything, emotions stirred up by both the women's liberation movement and the gay rights movement had raised the stakes for parents wanting to do the right thing. What "the right thing" might be was no clearer after a decade or so of sex role research and in-home experiments, and the battle lines were drawn between liberal and conservative parents in the modern culture wars. Conservative parents, as might be expected, argued in support of traditional, heteronormative masculinity and femininity, and they preferred clothing that reflected those values. Liberal parents were less predictable; some continued to seek out and purchase unisex clothing and reject strongly masculine and feminine styles. Others, especially those who had been children themselves during the 1970s, were less doctrinaire about the matter, letting their children be the final arbiters as they entered toddlerhood. Between conservative and liberal parents, of course, there were millions of parents who had no strong opinions on the matter at all.

Advances in prenatal testing and imaging technology that made it possible to know a fetus's sex long before birth affected all of these parents, regardless of their beliefs. Amniocentesis and ultrasound testing had been available for decades but rarely used because of the expense and risk involved. With the increase in the number of women over thirty-five having babies (especially first babies) and the introduction of less expensive technologies, prenatal screening became more common around 1985 and was routine by the second half of the 1990s. Detecting the sex of the fetus was never the primary goal, except in the case of sex-linked birth defects. The medical literature still contains the advice that ultrasound (sonogram) imaging is unnecessary in normal pregnancies, yet the "gender sonogram" (at about twenty weeks) is a hot topic in online pregnancy support groups.

No matter what their own beliefs on the matter of clothing and gender, late twentieth-century parents, most raised in child-centered, post-WWII households by parents who at least listened to their wishes and opinions, were inclined to share decisions about clothing with their children, if not defer to their tastes completely. The child consumer had been an important actor in American children's clothing since the early 1900s, but for most of that time the parents—particularly the mother—had been the child's agent, purchasing food, toys, and clothing on his or her behalf, until the child was old enough to have a say. It is impossible to say what that age might be, although the generational conflict over teenage fashions since 1920s suggests that parents preferred it to be later and adolescents pushed for earlier autonomy. Clearly, the shift to more masculine clothing for little boys between 1900 and 1920 can be attributed to the idea that the "emerging" manly nature of the boy would manifest itself in demands for less babyish, effeminate clothing. Anecdotal evidence and the rhetoric of advertising copy since the 1980s both point to a strong tendency to let boys and girls choose their own clothing as soon as they can point and say, "Dat one." In today's marketing environment, very young consumers must be taken into consideration when trying to understand their clothing. This is especially significant in light of evidence about gender identity formation in preschoolers and their perceptions of its possible impermanence. The more gender binary the children's clothing market becomes, the more it fits the worldview of the three- to five-year-old consumers looking for ways to express an unambiguous gender identity. The more parents let their children make their own clothing decisions, the more gender binary the clothing market will become.

Each of these factors alone would have been likely to result in more gendered baby and toddler clothing and fewer neutral choices. For all of them to converge at once, between 1985 and 1995, provided today's young adults with a unique set of lessons about sex, sexuality, and gender expression at a very young age. This chapter is their story, one that is still unfolding, as they become parents themselves.

THE "FAILURE" OF NONSEXIST CHILD REARING AND UNISEX CLOTHING

By the mid-1980s, public enthusiasm for nonsexist child rearing appeared to be waning or at least complicated by reality. Anecdotal evidence was spreading at playgroups and coffee breaks: the daughter who wanted to grow up to be "just a mommy" and told her physician-mother that "girls can't be doctors," and the son who bit his cheese slice into the shape of a gun and used his baby doll as a hammer. After a decade of entertaining the notion that gender identity was a consequence of nurture, the word from the parenting trenches was that nature was hard to deny. As Jesse Ellison (b. 1978) wrote:

> "We all thought that the differences had to do with how you were brought up in a sexist culture, and if you gave children the same chances, it would equalize," my mom says. "It took a while to think, 'Maybe men and women really are different from each other, and they're both equally valuable.'"[1]

Ellison remembers, "As soon as I could speak, I demanded they replace my overalls with a long, pink, lacy dress. Far from gender-neutral, I was emphatically, defiantly a 'girl.'" As a preteen in the 1970s, Pagan Kennedy was fascinated with the 1950s, which represented "a racy world of teen rituals, of well-defined gender roles and contact dancing," not the decade of conformity and repression rejected by so many baby boomers, who had experienced the reality of the Levittown years.[2]

Perhaps the best articulation of the adult view was Sara Bonnett Stein's 1983 book, *Girls and Boys: The Limits of Nonsexist Childrearing*. Stein admitted the value of giving both boys and girls a wide range of options of activities and clothing styles—she noted approvingly that tomboys in the 1970s did not stand out as much as they had in earlier generations—but for the most part she argued that trying to erase gender differences was at best a wasted effort and could do more harm than good. Our culture gave them the option of dressing in a way that did not signify gender; their program urged them to seek a form of clothing that *did* signify gender.

Stein's main argument was that gender identity is innate ("programmed"), and most of her evidence was anecdotal: very young children who insisted on traditional clothing, toys, and behavior despite their parents' efforts to the contrary. But she also was able to reference scientific studies that suggested physiological explanations for behavioral differences between boys and girls. The danger, she warned, was "confusion" (a topic to which she devoted an entire chapter), which could lead to homosexuality. Stein offered no explanation why nonsexist child rearing could benefit "tomboys" without leading to lesbianism while "confusing" effeminate boys and inclining them to homosexuality.

ADVICE BOOKS: SEPARATE (EQUAL?) ADVICE FOR PARENTING BOYS AND GIRLS

One of the signs that the unisex era of parenting was over was the appearance of gender-specific advice literature. The first to appear was *The Little Boy Book* (1986), promoted on its dust jacket as "the only book of its kind."[3] The back cover elaborates: "Yes, boys are different no matter what we've learned in the past decade about raising the 'unisex' child." The companion volume, *The Little Girl Book* (also "the only book of its kind") appeared six years later, and the contrast between them is instructive, beginning with the authors' promise to explain "how to provide a nonsexist environment for your daughter."[4] Parents of girls needed to learn "how girls acquire a sense of themselves as female," while apparently no equivalent lessons in masculinity were required to raise boys. The authors of the "girl" book emphasized the "diversity of today's" girls, and a basketball-toting girl wearing jeans and a polo shirt appeared on the cover with five other, more feminine images. The "boy" book's authors acknowledged some diversity in male behavior, but the cover images include no artists or dancers. Unsurprisingly, homosexuality receives five paragraphs of consideration in *The Little Boy Book* but none at all in *The Little Girl Book*. Beyond summarizing the research suggesting that homosexuality is probably innate, and noting that many feminine boys grow up to be gay, the authors offer no guidance to parents whose sons may not conform to the "typical" masculine behaviors (activity, aggression, independence) described in the book.

But was nonsexist child rearing a "failed experiment"? The unisex generation of girls grew up to believe they "could wear pink, spend money on fancy shoes, and simultaneously expect—no, demand—the same success as men."[5] Third-wave "feminine feminists" might confuse and frustrate their second-wave mothers with their appearance—and the way they dress their children—but many still embraced the core belief of equal opportunity for their sons and daughters. The complications seen in children's clothing are not superficial; they reflect the vexing choices and contradictions that exist in modern gender roles for adults.

BIRTH CONTROL, PREGNANCY TESTS, AND ULTRASOUND

In any discussion of babies and baby culture in the last generation, it would be foolish to ignore the medical and technological advances that transformed pregnancy. The introduction of safe, reliable contraceptives was the first of many innovations that transformed the entire process from one that seemed random and unpredictable into an experience that could be chosen, controlled, personalized, and commodified. It was not only motherhood that was affected; modern technology has essentially moved the beginning of babyhood from the moment of birth to an ever-earlier moment of individuation, in which gender plays a major role.

Although physical barriers such as condoms and diaphragms were available long before oral contraceptives were invented, there is general consensus that "the Pill" placed the power of choosing motherhood in the hands of individual women on an unprecedented scale. The legalization of abortion after *Roe v. Wade* further advanced the idea that giving birth was a personal choice, although choosing abortion has remained highly controversial. By the late 1970s, many young women were delaying childbearing or choosing to remain "child-free"—the preferred term to the more negative "childless." Elective tubal ligations and vasectomies added to the available options, should women or men wish to control their own reproduction permanently.[6] The age-old problem of infertility also faded for millions of couples, beginning with the 1978 birth of Louise Brown in the UK, the first in vitro ("test tube") baby.[7] Within a decade, a variety of methods, from surrogates to egg donation to "designer" sperm banks, offered more couples the opportunity to conceive and bear children.

None of these advances had a direct effect on baby and toddler fashions, except for possibly resulting in a smaller pool of hand-me-downs as family sizes shrank. However, a secondary effect of earlier, more accurate pregnancy testing and the growth of prenatal testing (particularly sonograms) radically changed what was known about the fetus—and when. We may think of human pregnancy as being nine months long, but the experience itself actually begins when the woman is aware she is carrying a child. Before modern testing methods, that was not likely to be a certainty until the end of the first trimester, and there are still cases of women who are unaware that they are pregnant until they go into labor. For most of the twentieth century, women who suspected they were pregnant could go to a doctor for a blood test and then typically waited two more weeks for the result. Just having one's period be a week or so late was not considered enough justification for the trip to the doctor; two missed periods were more of an indication, meaning that even in the 1950s and 1960s, women might be certain they were pregnant for six or seven months, not nine. *Our Bodies, Ourselves* (1973) reported that the best available test was not accurate until two weeks after the first missed period, with the results sometimes not available for another two weeks.

Pregnancy testing advanced swiftly in the late 1970s because of improvements in prenatal care and the availability of legal abortion, both strong arguments for early detection. The first breakthrough was in 1976, with FDA approval of e.p.t. This offered instant results, available in an at-home version as well as one for use in clinics and doctors' offices. Other brands quickly followed, including Predictor, Answer, and ACU-TEST. Tests with digital displays, which debuted in 2003, are easier to read but do not detect pregnancy any earlier. Effectively, women using home test kits since the late 1970s have experienced longer pregnancies than their mothers did—as much as two months longer.

Before the 1970s, doctors were very limited in their ability to monitor fetal development and detect abnormalities before birth. The emergence of fetal sonography (use of ultrasound technology to produce images of the baby while still in the womb) in the 1970s, followed by rapid improvements in image quality, cost, and portability, resulted in real gains in prenatal care, but this also opened the door to knowing the sex of the baby months before birth, which has had dramatic, nonmedical consequences.

Dr. Joseph Woo's website, The History of Ultrasound in Obstetrics and Gynecology, notes the influence of "both a 'Consumer Pull' and 'Technology Push'" in the expansion of ultrasound technology between 1975 and the early 1990s, when fetal scans at twenty weeks had become routine. By the time fast 3D scans became affordable in the late 1990s, it was clear that consumers were as interested in getting a sneak peek at their babies as they were in any medical indications. Woo expresses his skepticism with carefully placed quotation marks:

> Stuart Campbell at the St. Georges Hospital in London was one of the early proponents for the 3-D scan to be an important catalyst for mothers to bond to their babies. What are known as "re-assurance scans" and the perhaps misnamed "entertainment scans" have started to develop. The attraction of being able to look at the face of your baby before birth was enthusiastically reported in lay parenting and health magazines. Manufacturers had adopted an unprecedented "profit marketing" strategy to advertise to providers and "reverse marketing" strategy to advertise to consumers, particularly after the arrival of the 4-D (dynamic or motion 3-D) machines.[8]

Similarly, the American Pregnancy Association concludes that ultrasounds are "not a necessary part of prenatal care" unless there is a "medical concern."[9] In contrast, expectant mothers on pregnancy support message boards routinely refer to the twenty-week screening as "the gender ultrasound" or "gender sonogram."

> I haven't bought anything yet, but done lots of looking! I'm probably going to wait until the gender ultrasound before I really start buying a lot of clothes. I may pick up some blankets, etc. before. Though, I'm going shopping in August with one of my BFFs, so that may change![10]

The latest chapter in this story is the rapid growth of stand-alone 3D/4D Ultrasound centers, which provide viewing rooms with large screens and a spa-like atmosphere with no medical services at all. According to 4D-Ultrasounds.com, an online directory, their listings went from 2 centers in 2003 to over 250 in 2010.[11] Packages include still images, video DVD showing the fetus in motion, and viewing parties for friends and family.[12] One happy customer described her experience:

> To my pleasure and surprise the room was very spacious (larger than my own living room). There was soft music playing, candlelight, and a large comfortable bed for Cara [her daughter]. Best of all was the Giant Screen

on the wall with which to view the baby. Plus two other screens positioned so that no matter which way Cara was laying she could also watch the baby.[13]

Medical advice notwithstanding, prenatal testing, primarily ultrasound, has introduced another choice for expectant parents: whether or not to know the sex of the baby before birth. Sometimes knowing is unavoidable; genetic testing for sex-linked abnormalities or a clear image of the baby's genitals can remove all doubt. But in most cases, what was once revealed in the delivery room can now be known at about twenty weeks, approximately halfway through the pregnancy. According to entrepreneur Kelly Boyington, 41 percent of pregnant mothers in America choose not to know their baby's sex before birth, but she points out that there are regional variations—in Texas, where she lives, the proportion is only 21 percent.[14] The actual numbers are more complicated; in my own tabulation of thirty responses to the question "Should I find out my baby's gender?" on a Dallas–Fort Worth online message board, seven women (23 percent) said they had opted not to know. Of the twenty-three (77 percent) who said they had asked for the news, three said they would not find out with future babies, and five women had more than one child and had made different choices with each.

A close reading of the many rationales for their decisions helps round out our understanding of this trend. First, pregnancy today is likely to be a family affair, so partners and other children often have an influence on the choice:

DH wanted to be surprised, but I won.

DH wanted to find out with our first and I agreed if we didn't for our second.

[The baby's sibling] had a strong preference, so I wanted to be able to prepare her one way or the other.

[My daughter] wants to know if it is a boy or a girl and asks all the time. I do not think she understands you cannot tell so early on. He he.

None of the respondents specifically indicated that their need to know was closely tied to consumption and the desire to have the "right" clothing and other items, although several mentioned the importance of knowing the sex so they could "plan." The desire to know their baby as an individual, with sex being the key element, was another common reason offered:

> When I found out we were having a boy, it made it much more real to me and I felt closer to him in the womb. I also liked that we could start trying out names on him in the womb. My logic is it is just as great to be surprised at 20 weeks as at 40. Also it got me so excited for having a boy—I am sure I would have done the same if I were having a girl, but it got me in the "boy" mindset.

> I agree that it makes it more real to me. I can focus on names etc.

> I like to be able to use my baby's name as I talk to them in the womb.

Some women admitted to having a preference for a boy or a girl and finding out so they could "adjust" if they were disappointed or throw themselves into preparations if the baby was the "right" sex:

> We found out, but only because I very badly wanted a boy and was very anxious to find out.

> I had a strong preference and I wanted to be prepared if I didn't get what I was hoping for.

> I wanted a boy so badly that we had to find out so I could make sure I didn't pull a Drew Barrymore in *Riding in Cars with Boys*. Also being OCD I needed to plan and being afraid of showing an ounce of disappointment at the idea of pink, Barbies, and having to finally learn how to braid hair we had to find out!

> We found out with the first two because I wanted a girl REALLY badly and wanted to shop.

About half of the parents who chose not to find out tended to express feminist ideals: an aversion to gender-specific clothing and toys and an intention to avoid gender stereotypes in raising their child. This suggests that choosing not to know may be part of a larger constellation of life-style attitudes and behaviors.

> Our parenting style isn't much affected by a particular sex, so it wasn't a big deal anyway. (We cloth diaper, co-sleep, swaddle, baby wear, don't circum-

cise, etc. so clothing, bedding, decor, toys, etc., didn't have to be gender-specific.)

We waited with our first, and it was DH's big moment to go out to the waiting room and announce to the whole family all at the same time (parents had called both brothers on the phone, so they could hear it live as well). We have the announcement on video, and it makes me smile every time. We have considered finding out whenever we get pregnant again, because both of us are wanting a girl this time. However, in all honesty, we loved being team green (most of the time), and we don't have to worry about a shower or getting baby gear this time, so we'll probably be team green again.

We kept it a surprise because I insisted. DH wanted to know. I just felt that it seemed more "natural" not to know. I mean, for how many thousands of years have humans managed to have babies without the sonogram telling you that you're having a boy or girl?

One woman noticed this pattern in the thread and explained her "contradictory" desire to know the sex but avoid gender stereotypes:

I'm impatient, but I prefer gender neutral for most stuff. I guess I'm a contradiction. Ultimately, we found out we're having a girl. But I kinda don't want to tell everyone because I really don't like pink and I would prefer to keep it to a minimum.

Bloggers on the topic tend to go into greater detail and share their discussions and decisions with friends and strangers alike.

The nerd in me got excited at the prospect of abandoning all the gender constraints we would inevitably put on our preparations if we knew whether the babe was a boy or a girl. Operation baby was now a fun sociological experiment. How many gender baby barriers could we break down when decorating a nursery or buying baby clothes?[15]

There are so few real and big surprises in the world anymore that it's actually kind of nice to have something completely unknown and anticipated for nine full months. It's almost a liberating experience, being able to imagine our future with either a boy or a girl, at almost the same time.[16]

That is part of the reason why we decided not to find out the sex of the baby. I can't stand it when kids are stuck in one color.[17]

"GENDER ULTRASOUND," GENDERED CLOTHING, AND NEUTRAL STYLES

For many contemporary parents, the twenty-week sonogram signals the start of real shopping and gift showers, focused on the child's revealed sex. Contrast this outcome of the gender ultrasound with the pattern noted by *Earnshaw's* in 1973 that mothers purchased most of their baby's first clothes in the last trimester.[18] Those initial purchases were also likely to be modest, with another wave of clothing arriving when the little son or daughter was born. Today's parents not only start furnishing their offspring's wardrobe and nursery earlier, but they also buy more items ahead of time, armed with the knowledge of the child's sex. I wonder if the result of these preparations might not be parents who are more inclined to perceive and treat their babies as gendered creatures.

Given the ambivalence and controversy surrounding unisex child rearing, the persistence of traditional gender stereotypes and the availability of technologies that detected a baby's sex long before birth (in pregnancies that were "longer" by as much as two months), the sharp and sudden gendering of infants' clothing in the mid-1980s might have been predicted. The trade press does not remark on any of these trends, however, only on the changes in style. Girls' styles were not only more often pastel but featured elements such as ruffles, gathers, puffed sleeves, and lace trim, while boys' styles were plainer and were more likely to be fabricated in highly saturated colors. The disappearance—and recent signs of revival—of neutral styles reveal something else.

First, the rapidity with which neutral options vanished in 1985 and 1986 probably reflects the weakening of demand as the number of "leading edge" baby boomers giving birth declined and the proportion of younger women grew who were more affected by the 1970s than by the 1950s. The differences between these generations of women could be posited as the distinction between second-wave and third-wave feminism, but not all American women have been feminists. Just as when rompers appeared on the scene in the early twentieth century, and different babies might wear them for different reasons, many factors could account for the sudden popularity of strongly gendered clothing in the mid-1980s. The generational demographic shift is one, but within that shift there are other demographic changes that are beyond the scope of this book. For example, the impact of immigration from Asia or Latin

Toddler fashion, 2011, featuring multiple symbols to reinforce gender.
Courtesy of Simplicity Creative Group.

America is unknown, even though the former would have been large enough to influence trends in many urban areas in the 1970s and 1980s, and the latter has been significant in national markets since the 1990s. One has only to look at trends in food, from the local grocery store to neighborhood restaurants, to see how immigration has diversified our consumer culture.

Whatever the reason, the industry's response was to provide increasingly gendered styles for infants beginning in the early 1980s, followed within a few years by similar styles for toddlers. The decline in neutral styles reflects both shrinking demand and the result of competition for shelf space in children's departments and boutiques. There were still exceptions to this pattern; as late as the early 1990s, parents wanting tailored, unfussy styles for their daughters could select boys' styles from retailers such as Lands' End, and dressy boys' clothing in the southern United States still featured pastels, smocking, and embroidery well into the 1990s.[19] Momma's Boy—Daddy's Girl, a store in northern Virginia, even calls these styles "that unique look of southern clothing" and specializes in "difficult to find" boys' clothing and brother-sister outfits in the same style. But for the most part, mass market American infant and toddler clothing has reflected a very strong binary view of gender. According to Peggy Orenstein, this is no accident. While doing research for her 2011 book *Cinderella Ate My Daughter,* she interviewed a marketing executive from LeapFrog, which produces electronic learning toys, not clothing. The executive even named the phenomenon "the pink factor." LeapFrog—and evidently many other manufacturers—know that strongly gendered products for children—pink computers, Barbie tricycles, Buzz Lightyear lunch boxes—mean double sales in families with both boys and girls.

This has not been without difficulties. Fewer neutral styles mean fewer hand-me-downs, which means increasing costs for families with at least one child of each sex.[20] According to the parenting message boards, children's clothing swaps and hand-me-downs from outside the family— extended family and friends—are still a common solution. Cost is more of an issue in recent years with the deep recession, and discussions about the economic advantages of neutral clothing are now frequent in online communities.

The most vocal critics of the absence of neutral styles are those parents for whom gendered clothing is seen as detrimental to children's development, although their criticisms are often more nuanced. Concerns about girls are more frequent, echoing feminist advocates of unisex clothing decades ago. Parents worry that dressing their infant daughter in ultrafeminine clothing will result in her being treated differently by caregivers and strangers and set her on a path of dependency and obsession with appearance. For them, neutral clothing would at least buy them some time before popular culture would begin to influence the little girl's sense of self. Parents of boys are less active in online discussions of the topic, but they express similar concerns about clothing that perpetuates stereotypes about aggressive or destructive behavior. (Onesies printed with "Here comes trouble" are one example.)

As infants grow into toddlers, they have become active participants in the gender binary fashion show, much to the amusement, chagrin, or dismay of their parents. For boys and girls whose gender identity generally conforms to their biological sex, this participation is likely to be an enthusiastic embrace. These are the girls who insist on wearing nothing but pink and prefer dresses to any form of pants and the boys who clamor for buzz-cuts and ubiquitous sports imagery. One of the most puzzling questions raised by the gendered clothing of the last generation is "What about the others?" What about tomboys, the little girls who for decades could wear plain girls' styles or their brother's hand-me-downs without appearing out of the mainstream? (In a study of college-age women in the early 1970s, 78 percent described themselves as "tomboys" as children, although the age to which they referred was unclear.[21]) What about the one person in one hundred classified as "intersex," whose body differs from standard male or female and whose sense of identity may not conform to the gender chosen by the parents?[22] What about boys who, like tomboys, feel more comfortable in the clothing of the other sex, but for whom the English language has no positive term?[23] Certainly, one of the outcomes of a strong gender binary in children's clothing is the lack of expressive options for children whose identities may be more fluid or contrary to stereotyped images of masculinity and femininity.

Even parents of "girly" girls and "all-boy" boys are not always completely comfortable with the available options. One of the common laments in the post-unisex boy-raising literature is that boys' expressions and choices are so much more limited than girls'. In *Beyond Dolls & Guns*, Susan Hoy Crawford noted, "Boys are unnecessarily cheated out of exciting clothes," and she suggested that boys should be allowed more choices of color, texture, and pattern. In *The Complete Idiot's Guide to Raising Boys* (2008), Laurie and Barron Helgoe write, "We want our boys to have access to the emotional and social freedom girls enjoy. We want them to feel less pressure to be strong and in charge. We'd like them to feel more comfortable with their vulnerabilities." Parents with these and similar concerns may also be inclined to reject boys' clothing with aggressive or "troublemaker" images and inscriptions and to prefer brighter colors to the black-brown-gray palette that has dominated toddler boys' clothing in recent years.

For parents of girls, the most troubling aspects of their fashions in the last decade have been pinkification, princesses, and sexualization. When pink reemerged as a feminine color in the mid-1980s, it was one of many options, especially for toddlers. Throughout the 1990s, other colors shared the spotlight, including turquoise, purple, and other hues, both pastel and bright. In the early 2000s, pink became ubiquitous—not just in baby and toddler clothing but for girls and women of all ages, and not just for clothing but for cell phones, power tools, and other products once devoid of gender.[24] As discussed in the chapter "Pink Is for Boys," there are signs of backlash against the essentialized symbolism of pink in many of these markets. Blogger "Distracted Daddy" writes of his daughter, who is usually clad in pink: "Hopefully once she's no longer a baby and any stranger can guess her gender at 40 yards we can move on from this color."[25] A group of expectant mothers in the October 2010 Babies community quickly warmed to a discussion on alternatives:

> So I'm not a pink hater. I like pink. I wear pink and love little pink accessories and what not. My husband makes fun of me about it.

> With that said WHY is everything for baby girls pink? I go to the store and 99 percent of the girl clothes are pink, the accessories are pink, the toys are pink, everything is pink. It's not the ONLY girly color. I see neutral stuff in green and yellow but how about we see a green dress, or a blue girl's outfit, not just gender neutral. I'd love to find some purple stuff, pretty blues, etc. It's a little frustrating.

Commenters added suggestions for vendors and manufacturers carrying girls' clothing and added their own views. It is particularly interesting to note that their "pink fatigue" often has nothing to do with traditional gender roles:

I feel the same way! I get especially frustrated that almost all of the girls' bedding is pink. Pink and brown, hot pink and black, pink flowers, PINK! I'm trying to find a solid lilac bedding set, and I'm having no luck whatsoever unless I want to shell out a ton of money on a custom bedding set. Frustrating!

I am with you on the pink. I specifically look for other colors, but at most retail stores it is hard to find. On our registry for the baby items, I requested clothing colors other than pink if possible. I sew and have bought material and baby clothes patterns.

Ahh I completely agree with you. The second I told my sister-in-law that I was having a girl, she was like "Oh, so now you can get all pink stuff!!" and I said, "Actually, we still like gender-neutral colors. We don't want all pink things." And she looked at me like I was crazy! I like pink, but I think they should make cute girls' clothes in ALL colors, not just pink or every shade of pink!

I mean, us women don't wear pink all the time, what about, orange, yellow, brown, blue, green, etc? I am so annoyed that the boys get all the blue stuff. I have some blue things that don't scream boy that I am keeping to use for my daughter. If it was me, I'd wear them, so why not?

PRINCESSES AND PAGEANTS

In 2001, Disney struck gold by rebranding its most popular animated heroines as "Disney Princesses" and launching a line of products for girls ages three to six. According to an interview with Peggy Orenstein, Disney executive Andy Mooney realized the potential market for princess paraphernalia after attending his first "Disney on Ice" performance. Seeing hundreds of little girls arriving for the show decked out in homemade princess outfits, "The light bulb went off. Clearly there was latent demand here. So the next morning I said to my team, 'O.K., let's establish standards and a color palette and talk to licensees and get as much product out there as we possibly can that allows these girls to do what they're doing anyway: projecting themselves into the characters from the classic movies.'" Orenstein was searching for the appropriate response to her own three-year-old daughter's fascination with Cinderella. Was princess play a harmless, meaningless activity? Natural and necessary? A gateway to eating disorders and second-class citizenship? As a child of the 1970s, Orenstein mused, "Maybe I'm still surfing a washed-out second wave of feminism in a third-wave world. Maybe princesses are in fact a sign of progress, an indication that girls can embrace their predilection for pink without compromising strength or ambition; that, at long last, they can 'have it all.'"[26]

Certainly, princess folktales are practically universal. In America, princess dress-up play predates Walt Disney's birth, not just his films. Modern critics are aware of this history and point to recent developments that may be less benign, mainly the commodification of the princess fantasy and the sexualization of girls' culture that it promotes. Child development scholars have noted the potential of modern, mass-produced amusements to "script" and restrict imaginative play. A girl with a homemade princess costume is theoretically freer to invent her own story line than a girl with a Disney Ariel or Jasmine costume who has seen the movies dozens of times. These story lines contain both empowering messages (overcoming obstacles, for example) and messages that parents may find disturbing (the importance of appearance, finding "Prince Charming" as a supreme goal).

Developmentally, it is very hard to deny the importance of fantasies that provide outlets for children to explore and understand their identities, especially the naturalness of play that helps them play "grown-up." Parental discomfort with Disney Princesses, Power Rangers, and other commercial identities is that they sometimes represent stereotypes that seem narrow compared with our more expansive dreams for our children.

The "beauty culture" aspect of princess play, in particular, raises concerns about the premature sexualization of children that our Victorian ancestors would find quite familiar. As described in chapter 1, one of the reasons for delaying gender distinctions in children's clothing was the fear that it would lead to premature awareness of sex. Modern parents may have positive feelings about pink and blue baby clothes and ruffled overalls for girls, but some have expressed growing concern about the trend for preadolescents, even very young children, to adopt gender expressions that are adult and sexual.

Perhaps nowhere is this as evident as in the world of children's beauty pageants. Beautiful baby contests are generations old, having been popular features of local and regional fairs in the nineteenth century, and beauty pageants in the modern sense appeared early in the twentieth century with the Miss America contest. The combination of beautiful baby contests with pageant-style competitions, complete with costumes, performances, sashes, and tiaras, coincided with the reemergence of traditional feminine styling for adults and children in the early 1980s.[27] The 1996 murder of six-year-old pageant star Jon Benet Ramsey brought children's pageants into the national spotlight and raised the issue of whether beauty contests for babies and preschoolers are appropriate. The pro-pageant argument is that it builds self-esteem and self-confidence and is an enjoyable family activity, as long as the child is not forced or under stress. Critics point to the heavy makeup, scanty costumes, and flirtatious routines and speculate on possible connections between pedophilia and images of baby beauty queens.[28] Since 2009, much of the public conversation about beauty pageants has centered around two television reality shows, *Toddlers and Tiaras* (TLC) and *Little Miss Perfect* (WE tv). In both cases, the networks claim to offer the series as "documenting" a current phenomenon and letting the audience draw their own conclusions. The shows' success is apparently based on a mix of true pageant fans and anti-pageant viewers who can't stand the parents, feel sorry for the girls, and can't change the channel because it's all too fascinating. (Not to mention reaffirming of their own superiority as parents.)

Similar concerns have been raised about clothing lines that offer sexy, trendy styles for very little girls. The most recent example is skinny jeans in infant sizes. But before that it was thong underpants for toddlers.[29] While the term "prostitots" was originally coined to refer to preteen girls who sported sexy fashions to emulate Britney Spears and Beyoncé Knowles, in recent years it has appeared more frequently in news articles and blog posts about clothing and toys for girls under six.[30] Nor are boys exempt; as this book was being written, Huggies introduced denim-look diapers with a commercial featuring a toddler boy, clad in only a shirt and diaper, "strutting" down the street and climbing into a convertible, as adults of both sexes admire his fashion sense. The voice-over is an adult male announcing, "I poo in blue." The commercial attracted national attention, with viewers weighing in on all sides of its appropriateness. Blogger Brooke Pollard noted, "In my opinion, the music and the staging are somewhat sexy—too sexy for a child to be in it," and the readers on her hospital-sponsored mothers' support site agree almost unanimously, with comments such as:

> It almost crosses the line into child porn. I mean seriously why would grown women be looking at a baby like that?

> Isn't child pornography about a child dressed to look sexy and beyond their age? In that case, that applies here, as we see women AND men ogling this little boy, who has been trained to look over his back in a very sexy manner.[31]

Danica Lo, of the fashion and shopping blog "Racked," pegged the reaction most accurately in her title "The Denim Huggies Diaper Commercial Is Creepy and Genius," and her comments lean overwhelmingly toward the "genius" category. Similarly, the comments on the Huggies channel on YouTube are mostly positive, and commenters who post criticisms are ridiculed for having dirty minds and no sense of humor.

Who is right? The Huggies boy is far from the first baby to be endowed with adult mannerisms for comic effect. Recent research on the effects of mass media and advertising on children, especially preadolescent girls, has resulted in a growing body of literature connecting popular culture and early sexual activity, body image anxiety, and eating disorders. How the media image of the savvy, street-smart, sexualized baby affects adult perceptions of infants and children is well beyond the scope of a book on the history of clothing, but an examination of children's fashions over the last generation suggests that the line between gender-appropriate and sexually attractive has become decidedly blurred. In the early 1990s, swimsuits for baby girls were almost always one-piece; femininity was expressed through color, floral prints, and ruffles. In the summer of 2010, on one shopping website that aggregates items from multiple sources, a third of the girls' bathing suits in sizes 0–12 months were two-piece styles, nearly all of them bikinis.[32] On an adult woman, it is safe to assume that a bikini is intended to be sexually attractive, if not provocative. What does it "mean" on a six-month-old? Even if it is just chosen to be cute or humorous, it connects an image associated with adult sexuality with design elements that simply convey femininity. Similarly, boys' clothing, while not designed to display their bodies in a sexualized fashion—typically they are loose-fitted and not especially revealing—have begun to sport sayings that characterize the wearer as sexually precocious. ("Chick Magnet," "I'm a Boob Man," and "Your Crib or Mine?" are available on the Hooters Gear website on infant bibs and onesies.) Unsurprisingly, the sexual messages on baby and toddler clothing are, without exception, heteronormative. Despite the widespread visibility of gays and lesbians in American culture and the growing public acceptance of marriage equality and other civil rights, it seems clear that clothing manufacturers and consumers routinely conflate sex and sexuality.

SIGNS OF CHANGE

One of the drawbacks of writing a history that brings the reader up to the present is that "the present" is a blurry, moving target. The other is that doing so draws the eye toward the future, tempting the author either to wait to write the next chapter (which I have already done, since 1987) or attempt to predict the future, which is not usually the historian's strong suit. In this last section, I will instead note some phenomena that might be signs of change, knowing that by the time the book is published, readers may be able to look around them and see what has actually happened.

The first trend is an apparent increase in the demand for—and availability of—neutral clothing for infants. This may coincide with a shift in the number of parents who are opting not to know the sex of their baby before birth, but statistics are hard to find and verify at this point. At any rate, over the last year, a search alert for "gender-neutral clothing" has delivered a growing number of personal blogs and shopping sites featuring that term. Gender-neutral styles for toddlers and children, however, are still few and far between. What constitutes "neutral" also does not seem to have changed much at all; the design vocabulary for children's clothing is still gender binary and fairly rigid.

One glaring exception to this inflexible gender code, oddly enough, is the color pink. It is possible now to buy pink dress shirts for toddler boys, just like those currently in fashion for adults. Royal Baby Boutique ("For your little prince or princess") offers a pink pacifier with the inscription "Momma's Boy."[33] This ironic, humorous use of pink might be the work of the babies of the 1980s, just now reaching parenthood and playing *with* the rules rather than by them.

One of my most persistent questions has been "How do gender rules affect children who do not conform to dominant gender expectations, or who are born intersex, or who grow up anything but heterosexual?" I

The resurgence of neutral options. "It's a baby!" White
onesie with red and black design, 2010.

Courtesy of LGBabyt.com, LGBabyT: The alternative to Pink&Blue.

am convinced that clothing does *not* "make the man" when it comes to
babies and toddlers; there is no evidence whatsoever that homosexuality
is any more or less prevalent now than it was when boys wore dresses
until they were five or that lesbianism spiked among the first generation
of girls to wear pants. But that does not mean that children between one
and six may not use clothing to help explore and express their biological
sex in the cultural landscape into which they were born. What is recent

and very interesting is the emergence of blogs, both personal and institutional, that support parents with gender nonconforming or gender variant children, mainly boys.

Author Sarah Hoffman writes about her son, Sam (she uses pseudonyms for herself and family members):

> He wore a dress to preschool, spent years pretending he was a princess, and now, as a second-grader, he has long flowing hair and a pink canopy over his bed. He is a pink boy. Like a tomboy, only different.[34]

Bedford Hope is the father of two sons, one of whom he describes as a "tomgirl" and who is about to enter middle school. Writing in response to a parent of a six-year-old boy who "likes girl things," he observes:

> You should tell your young son that there are many many boys like him, who like girl things. Sometimes these feelings are very strong and last forever, and there are ways that boys can become girls when they are older, but very often boys who like girl things come to accept their own bodies and find friends like themselves and have good lives with friends and families.[35]

Parenting literature is also starting to address the question of gender variant children, although the emphasis is usually on boys, not girls. Does your preschool son indulge in cross-dressing? Laurie and Barron Helgoe attempt to defuse anxiety about dress-up play at this age, but leave the door open for the possibility that it may be more than a stage:

> If he does feel uncomfortable with his gender, he will let you know in more obvious ways—he'll insist that he is not a boy or that he does not want to be a boy. If he truly seems uncomfortable with his gender, you can reassure him that boys and girls can do a lot of the same things. Help him develop his identity as a person and not only as a boy.[36]

Furthermore, when the authors discuss puberty and sexuality (Boy Gets Hormones), they offer a very matter-of-fact, supportive discussion of gay boys, not even mentioning the conservative belief that homosexuality is a choice, a "lifestyle," or reversible.

The story of gendered clothing for our youngest children is still unfolding and will probably never be finished. Each generation learns a new set of rules, devised by the grown children of the previous generation. Each wave of parents dress their sons and daughters in ways that represent their own memories and their present lives as men and women.

Babies initially grow up in their parents' cultures, but by toddlerhood they are producing their own, changing the cultural environment by their very presence. Someday babies may be perceived more as "persons" and less as "boys" and "girls," just as they were generations ago, but that has not been our trajectory for more than one hundred years. In the meantime, if anyone wants to observe the most obvious, seemingly immutable gendered aspects of our culture, visit a class of four-year-olds. Existing in the time between awareness of their sex and security in its expression, they apply every rule they observe with uncanny precision. By the time they reach their teens, they will be twisting and stretching the rules that vex them the most. Then they will become adults (and parents), and the dance will go on.

NOTES

1. UNDERSTANDING CHILDREN'S CLOTHING

1. Connell, *Gender,* 8.

2. Fausto-Sterling et al., "How Sexually Dimorphic Are We?"

3. The current clinical term for this is "gender variant"; in the humanities, the term "gender queer" is sometimes used. Associated slang terms include "tomboy" and "sissy."

4. Careful description of overlooked categories of artifacts is an essential first step for analyzing patterns and changes in their design, use, and meaning. I hope that this book will draw at least some costume historians away from the glamour of fashion and encourage more research into everyday clothing, especially of men and boys.

5. Wehrle and Paoletti, "What Do We Wear to the Wedding Now That the Funeral Is Over?"

6. Kett, "Adolescence and Youth in Nineteenth-Century America," 287.

7. Dawson, "The Miniaturizing of Girlhood: Nineteenth-Century Playtime and Gendered Theories of Development."

8. Cook, *Symbolic Childhood.*

9. For more on John Money's research, consult his own work, especially *Man and Woman, Boy and Girl* (1972) and the autobiography of his most famous patient, John Colapinto (*As Nature Made Him: The Boy Who Was Raised as a Girl* (2000).

10. Steele, "The F-Word."

11. Brooks-Gunn, *He & She: How Children Develop Their Sex-Role Identity,* 97–125.

12. Bem, "Gender Schema Theory and Its Implications for Child Development."

13. Maccoby and Jacklin, *The Psychology of Sex Differences.*

14. Maccoby, *The Two Sexes,* 166–67.

15. Ibid., 173.

16. Ibid., 227–28.

17. Boston and Levy, "Changes and Differences in Preschoolers' Understanding of Gender Scripts."

18. Harris, "Where Is the Child's Environment? A Group Socialization Theory of Development."

19. Kaiser, "Sex Typing in Dress: A Developmental Approach."

20. This concept has been variously attributed to J. C. Flugel and James Laver. According to Fred Davis in *Fashion, Culture, and Identity,* 83, Flugel described the phenomena but did not use the phrase, and Laver used the phrase, attributing it only to "some psychologists."

21. U.S. Census Bureau, "1951–1994 Statistical Abstracts," http://www.census.gov/prod/www/abs/statab1951–1994.htm.

2. DRESSES ARE FOR GIRLS AND BOYS

1. Cook, *Commodification of Childhood,* 85.

2. Calvert, *Children in the House,* 91.

3. Fine, *Delusions of Gender.*

4. According to the *Oxford English Dictionary,* the word "toddle" as a description of an uncertain, wide-stanced gait dates back to the sixteenth century, but "toddler" was not used to refer to a child until the nineteenth century.

5. Ariès, *Centuries of Childhood.*

6. Warwick, Pitz, and Wyckoff, *Early American Dress.*

7. Jordan, *The Call of the Twentieth Century.*

8. Roosevelt, "What Can We Expect of the American Boy."

9. Kett, "Adolescence and Youth in Nineteenth-Century America."

10. Cook, *Symbolic Childhood.*

11. Cook, *Commodification of Childhood,* 67.

12. W. D. Stauffer & Co. trade card 6x72.26, Winterthur Museum and Library, Joseph Downs Collection of Manuscripts and Printed Ephemera.

13. *McLaughlin XXXX Coffee Paper Doll,* Winterthur Museum and Library.

14. Warwick, Pitz, and Wyckoff, *Early American Dress.*

15. Harrington, "The Southerner's Daughter."

16. Jensen, "The Economics of Intended Re-use."

17. Wishy, *Child and the Republic,* 14.

18. Robinson, *Loom and Spindle.*

19. "The Nursery."

20. "Children's Dresses."

21. "Questions and Answers."

22. "Boys' Clothing."

3. PANTS ARE FOR BOYS AND GIRLS

1. Cook, *Commodification of Childhood,* 85–87.
2. Clare Rose, letter to author, November 16, 1987.
3. John Price Griffith, *The Care of the Baby,* 164.
4. Ibid., 101.
5. "Boys' Suits," 425.
6. "Rompers for Boys or Girls," 214.
7. Ibid., 301.
8. "Bloomer Dress," 205.
9. "Creepers," 278.
10. Griffith, *The Care of the Baby,* 112.
11. Betty Bobs family, Pictorial Review 1925, 74x438.362, Winterthur Museum and Library.
12. Cook, *Commodification of Childhood,* 17. Cook uses the term "menti-fact" for this concept, crediting anthropologist Ray W. Birdwhistle for the very useful concept for a "discursively configured" reality, as opposed to a physical artifact.

4. A BOY IS NOT A GIRL

The epigraph is from a nursery rhyme attributed to English poet Robert Southey (1774–1843), ca. 1820.

1. The gender rules for girls' clothing changed much less during the same period, except for the adoption of rompers and other trousered styles already discussed in the previous chapter, "Pants Are for Boys and Girls, and the move to distinguish them from boys, effectively eliminating most neutral styles, did not occur until the 1980s.
2. Alcott, *The Young Mother,* 83; William Dewees, *A Treatise on the Physical and Medical Treatment of Children,* 250.
3. Dickens, *Sketches by Boz,* 56.
4. Paoletti, "Ridicule and Role Models as Factors in American Men's Fashion Change, 1880–1910."
5. Thwaite, *Waiting for the Party,* 95.
6. Burnett, *Little Lord Fauntleroy,* 17.
7. "Who Controls Fauntleroy?" *New York Times,* February 5, 1889.
8. Burnett, *The Romantick Lady,* 173.
9. "The Theatres."
10. "Little Lord Fauntleroy." *New York Times,* December 4, 1888.
11. Yum Yum, "The Letter-Box."
12. Maurice, "Best Sellers of Yesterday."

13. "Mrs. Deland's *Awakening of Helena Richie*." 116.

14. Beard, "How to Cross a Stream on a Log."

15. The difference between "knickerbockers" and "knickers" was mainly fullness. Knickerbockers, based on full seventeenth-century Dutch trousers, fell out of use for boys ages two through four and were replaced by knickers (less full and gathered into a cuff at the knee) or short pants with no gathers.

16. Beffel, "The Fauntleroy Plague."

17. "Boy of Today Is Not a Fauntleroy."

18. Senior Men's Group, Prince Georges Plaza, "What Did You Wear?"

19. Grant, "A 'Real Boy' and Not a Sissy: Gender, Childhood, and Masculinity, 1890–1940."

20. "Child Study."

21. "The Home Club."

22. Hall, "New Lights on Childhood," 585.

23. Beard, "How to Cross a Stream on a Log."

24. Johnson, "The Problems of Boyhood: A Course of Ethics for Boys in the Sunday School."

25. Jesse Bering, "One Reason Why Humans Are Special and Unique: We Masturbate. A Lot," *Bering in Mind* (blog), June 22, 2010, http://www.scientificamerican.com/blog/post.cfm?id=one-reason-why-humans-are-special-a-2010-06-22.

26. Hall, "How and When to Be Frank with Boys."

27. Hall, "The Feminist in Science."

28. Randolph, *A Shower of Verses.*

29. Hall, "New Lights on Childhood," 577.

30. Boorman, *Developing Personality in Boys.*

31. University Society, *The Child Welfare Manual: A Handbook of Child Nature and Nurture for Parents and Teachers,* 1:255.

32. Ibid., 1:254.

33. Croy, *1,000 Things a Mother Should Know with Reference to Tiny Babies and Growing Children.*

34. Curtis, "What to Make for a Boy."

35. Hall, "New Lights on Childhood," 577.

5. PINK IS FOR BOYS

1. "Pink or Blue?"

2. Janea Whitacre, personal correspondence, October 30, 2008.

3. Worrell, *Children's Costume in America, 1607–1910.*

4. "Infants' Clothing," 103.

5. Chalmers, "Dressmaking Made Easy—The Layette."

6. Hooper, "Hints on Home Dressmaking," January 1893.

7. One yet-unsubstantiated suggestion is that some African American mothers preferred lavender to pink or blue.

8. "Fashions: Baby's Clothes."

9. Jeanne Jennings, personal correspondence, 2010. Jeanne's daughter (b. 1982) was given blue clothing by an elderly Swiss friend, who said it was the traditional girl color. My son received two pink onesies from Korean graduate students in 1986.

10. Callahan and Paoletti, *Is It a Boy? Is It a Girl?*

11. Birthday cakes were often described or pictured in baby books, and nearly always had white, pink, or pink and white frosting.

12. Pink was also associated strongly enough with girls that the first "Baby X" study of adult reactions to a baby's sex used the colors of overalls to "change" the baby's apparent sex: pink for "Beth," blue for "Adam." Culp, "A Comparison of Observed and Reported Adult-Infant Interactions: Effects of Perceived Sex."

13. "Bringing Back Mak."

14. Hall, "New Lights on Childhood."

15. Ellison, "My Parents' Failed Experiment in Gender Neutrality."

16. Hurlbert and Ling, "Biological Components of Sex Differences in Color Preference."

17. Ann Limpert, "Is Pink the New Blue?"

6. UNISEX CHILD REARING AND GENDER-FREE FASHION

1. I specifically use "unisex" to refer to clothing from this period, and "neutral" or "ungendered" for clothing that could be worn by both boys and girls from other time periods. The term, which was coined in the 1960s and applied widely to clothing, hairstyles, bathrooms, and many other objects, is as much an artifact of its time as the styles themselves.

2. "Holiday Forecast."

3. Raphael, "How to Sell Infants and Toddler Wear," 33.

4. E. Culp. "A Comparison of Observed and Reported Adult-Infant Interactions: Effects of Perceived Sex." Sex Roles 9 (1983).

5. Marlo Thomas and Letty Cottin Pogrebin, "The History of Free to Be You and Me," http://www.freetobefoundation.org/.

6. Wilson, "Marlo Thomas: 'Free to Be' for You and Me, 35 Years Later."

7. Wyden, "When Both Wear the Pants."

8. Gibralter, "Reconsidering Dresses: If Dresses Are Dead, Then Why Are They Selling?"

9. "A New Day Dawning at Sears."

10. "The Power of a Frilly Apron: Coming of Age in Sodom and New Milford."

11. Geoffrey Montgomery, "Color Blindness: More Prevalent among Males," 2008, http://www.hhmi.org/senses/b130.html.

7. GENDERED AND NEUTRAL CLOTHING SINCE 1985

1. Ellison, "My Parents' Failed Experiment in Gender Neutrality."

2. Kennedy, *Platforms: A Microwaved Cultural Chronicle of the 1970s.*

3. Moore and Frost, *The Little Boy Book: A Guide to the First Eight Years.*

4. Laskin and O'Neill, *The Little Girl Book: Everything You Need to Know to Raise a Daughter Today.*

5. Ellison, "My Parents' Failed Experiment in Gender Neutrality."

6. These procedures were initially considered permanent; since the 1980s, surgical reversals have been easier and more common.

7. "Medicine: Test-Tube Baby: It's a Girl."

8. Woo, "History of Ultrasound in Obstetrics and Gynecology, Part 1," http://www.ob-ultrasound.net/history1.html.

9. "Ultrasound: Sonogram."

10. Melanie, "Have You Started Buying Baby Clothes Yet?" *JustMommies Message Boards,* July 4, 2010, http://www.justmommies.com/forums/f1454-due-date-club-february-2011/2031718-have-you-started-buying-baby-clothes-yet.html.

11. "4D Ultrasound, 3D Ultrasound or Sonogram, Ultrasound Provider Directory," http://www.4d-ultrasounds.com/.

12. "Welcome to First Glimpse 3D Ultrasounds and Prenatal Massage," http://www.firstglimpse3d.com/ultrasound_massage.html.

13. "3D & 4D Ultrasound—Fairfax, Virginia—Washington, D.C.," http://www.3dand4d.com/.

14. "What Is NFO," http://www.notfindingout.com/store/pages .php?pageid=16.

15. Alaine, "Gender Neutral=Only Yellow & Green Need Apply."

16. Tom Coffee, "The 9 Month Wait: The Case for Not Finding Out the Gender of a Baby," *Spilling Coffee* (blog), July 11, 2010, http://www.spilling-coffee.com/2010/07/11/the-9-month-waitthe-case-for-not-finding-out-the-gender-of-a-baby/.

17. "Pink Pink Pink (mild vent)," http://www.whattoexpect.com/forums/october-2010-babies/topic/pink-pink-pink-mild-vent.

18. "Selling Infants' Clothing," 41.

19. Searches on smocked boys' rompers over the last two years routinely turn up manufacturers and retailers of these items, mostly located in Texas, Florida, and other southern states.

20. "Will I Have a Boy or a Girl?" *Baby Bedding,* http://www.twin babybedding.org/will-i-have-a-boy-or-a-girl-will-you-have-a-baby-boy-or-baby-girl.

21. "What Are Little Girls Made of? Puppy Dogs' Tails, Too."

22. "How Common Is Intersex? Intersex Society of North America," http://www.isna.org/faq/frequency.

23. Besides the common term "sissy," I have found the terms "sissy boy," "pink boy," "girly boy," and "tomgirl." Clinical or scholarly terms (gender variant, gender nonconforming, transgender or gender dysphoric) are also used as nonslang equivalents.

24. The film *Legally Blonde* popularized the phrase "pink is the new black," and protagonist Elle is the contradictory fashionista blonde with brains. Her head-to-toe pink wardrobe contrasts with the dull, professional wardrobes of the other female law students.

25. "Pink Is the New Everything," *Distracted Daddy* (blog), June 7, 2010, http://www.distracteddaddy.com/reflections/pink-is-the-new-everything.

26. Orenstein, "What's Wrong With Cinderella?"

27. *Pageant Magazine,* the leading industry publication, debuted in January 1980, at a time when, according to its own history, interest in pageants was on the decline due to the women's rights movement.

28. Robin, "Should Toddler Beauty Pageants Be Banned?" *Opinion Matters,* June 23, 2009, http://www.floridatoday.com/content/blogs/opinion /2009/06/should-toddler-beauty-pageants-be.shtml; Boles, "Pedophilia and Child Beauty Pageant Perversion."

29. Erin Donnelly, "Skinny Jeans for Infants, Toddlers a Hot Trend," *Stylelist,* http://www.stylelist.com/2010/08/13/skinny-jeans-infants-toddlers/; Cristina Mohr, "Does the Prosti-tot Fashion Trend Encourage Danger to Young Girls?" *Helium,* n.d., http://www.helium.com/ items/1353422-prosti-tots-prostitots-prosti-tot-prostitot-sexualization-of-little-girls.

30. "Prostitots," *All or Nothing at All,* July 20, 2009, http://heidi21678 .blogspot.com/2009/07/prostitots.html.

31. Pollard, "Huggies Crosses the Line (Video)."

32. See http://www.shopstyle.com.

33. "Personalized Pacifiers™ Pink Mommas Boy Baby Pacifier Binkie."

34. Sarah Hoffman, "On Parenting a Boy Who Is Different," *Sarah Hoffman* (blog), http://www.sarahhoffmanwriter.com/sarah-hoffmans-blog/.

35. Bedford Hope, "Letter to a Concerned Parent of a Gender Variant Six-Year-Old," *Accepting Dad* (blog), April 9, 2010, http://www.acceptingdad .com/2010/04/09/letter-to-a-concerned-parent-of-a-gv-six-year-old/.

36. Helgoe and Helgoe, *The Complete Idiot's Guide to Raising Boys.*

BIBLIOGRAPHY

ARCHIVAL SOURCES

Indiana State Museum, Indianapolis (children's clothing)
Indianapolis Children's Museum (paper dolls, children's magazines, children's clothing)
Museum of the Rockies, Bozeman, Mont. (children's clothing)
Strong Museum of Play, Rochester, N.Y. (paper dolls and related materials)
University of California Los Angeles Louise M. Darling Biomedical Library History and Special Collections for the Sciences (baby record books)
University of Maryland Historic Costume and Textiles Collection (children's clothing, photographs)
Valentine Richmond History Center, Richmond, Va. (children's clothing)
Winterthur Museum and Library, Joseph Downs Collection of Manuscripts and Printed Ephemera, Wilmington, Del. (paper dolls and related materials)

PUBLISHED SOURCES

Alaine, Julie. "Gender Neutral = Only Yellow & Green Need Apply." *This Beloved Life,* July 10, 2010.
Alcott, William. *The Young Mother.* Boston: Light & Stearns, 1836.
Ariès, Philippe. *Centuries of Childhood.* London: Pimlico, 1996.
"The Baby's Outfit." *Delineator,* July 1896.
Beard, Dan. "How to Cross a Stream on a Log." *Outing, an Illustrated Monthly Magazine of Recreation,* July 1904.
Beffel, John Nicholas. "The Fauntleroy Plague." *Bookman,* April 1927.
Bem, Sandra Lipsitz. "Androgyny vs. the Tight Little Lives of Fluffy Women and Chesty Men." *Psychology Today,* September 1975.
———. "Gender Schema Theory and Its Implications for Child Development: Raising Gender-Aschematic Children in a Gender-Schematic Society." *Signs* 8 (Summer 1983): 598–616.
Blumer, Herbert. "Fashion: From Class Differentiation to Collective Selection." *Sociological Quarterly* 10, no. 3 (1969): 275–91.

Boles, David W. "Pedophilia and Child Beauty Pageant Perversion." *Urban Semiotic,* August 18, 2006.

Boorman, W. Ryland. *Developing Personality in Boys.* New York: Macmillan, 1929.

Boston, M. B., and G. D. Levy. "Changes and Differences in Preschoolers' Understanding of Gender Scripts." *Cognitive Development* 6 (1991): 412–17.

"Boy of Today Is Not a Fauntleroy." *New York Times,* November 16, 1924, sec. 4.

"Boys and Girls." *Harper's Magazine,* December 1876, 19.

"Boys' Clothing." *Harper's Bazaar,* December 20, 1890.

"Boys' Dresses." *Vogue Patterns,* October 1937.

"Boys' Suits," Sears, Roebuck & Co. catalog, Fall 1910.

Bridges, William E. "Family Patterns and Social Values in America, 1825–1875." *American Quarterly* 17, Spring (1965): 3–11.

"Bringing Back Mak." *Earnshaw's Infants, Girls and Boys Wear Review*, April 1988.

Brooks-Gunn, Jeanne. *He & She: How Children Develop Their Sex-Role Identity.* Englewood Cliffs, N.J.: Prentice-Hall, 1979.

Burnett, Frances Hodgson. *Little Lord Fauntleroy.* New York: Charles Scribner's Sons, 1887.

Burnett, Vivian. *The Romantick Lady.* New York: Charles Scribner's Sons, 1927.

Burnham, Dorothy K. *Cut My Cote.* Toronto: Royal Ontario Museum, 1973.

Callahan, Colleen, and Jo B. Paoletti. *Is It a Boy? Is It a Girl?* Richmond, Va.: Valentine Museum, 1999.

Calvert, Karin Lee Fishbeck. *Children in the House: The Material Culture of Early Childhood, 1600–1900.* Boston: Northeastern University Press, 1992.

Carmichael, Carrie. *Non-sexist Childraising.* Boston: Beacon Press, 1977.

Chalmers, Eleanore, "Dressmaking Made Easy—The Layette." *Delineator,* February 1911.

"Child Study." *New York Times,* August 8, 1895.

"Children's Dresses." *Peterson's Magazine,* February 1885.

Colapinto, John. *As Nature Made Him: The Boy Who Was Raised as a Girl.* New York: HarperCollins, 2000.

Connell, R. W. *Gender.* Malden, Mass.: Blackwell, 2002.

Cook, Daniel. *The Commodification of Childhood: The Children's Clothing Industry and the Rise of the Child Consumer.* Durham, N.C. : Duke University Press, 2004.

———. *Symbolic Childhood.* New York: Peter Lang, 2002.

Crawford, Susan. *Beyond Dolls & Guns: 101 Ways to Help Children Avoid Gender Bias.* Portsmouth, N.H.: Heinemann, 1996.

"Creepers." Sears, Roebuck & Co. catalog, Spring 1913, 278.

Cross, Gary S. *The Cute and the Cool: Wondrous Innocence and Modern American Children's Culture.* Oxford: Oxford University Press, 2004.

———. *Kids' Stuff: Toys and the Changing World of American Childhood.* Cambridge, Mass.: Harvard University Press, 1999.

———. *Time and Money: The Making of Consumerist Modernity.* New York: Routledge, 1993.

Croy, Mae Savell. *1,000 Things a Mother Should Know with Reference to Tiny Babies and Growing Children.* New York: G. P. Putnam's Sons, 1917.

Culp, E. "A Comparison of Observed and Reported Adult-Infant Interactions: Effects of Perceived Sex," *Sex Roles* 9 (1983).

Curtis, Helen Perry. "What to Make for a Boy." *Parents,* October 1932.

Davis, Fred. *Fashion, Culture, and Identity.* Chicago: University of Chicago Press, 1994.

Dawson, Melanie. "The Miniaturizing of Girlhood: Nineteenth-Century Playtime and Gendered Theories of Development." In *The American Child: A Cultural Studies Reader,* ed. Caroline F. Levander and Carol J. Singley. New Brunswick, N.J.: Rutgers University Press, 2003.

Dearborn, George Van Ness. *The Psychology of Clothing.* Princeton: Psychological Review Co., 1918.

Dewees, William. *A Treatise on the Physical and Medical Treatment of Children.* Philadelphia: Carey, Lea & Blanchard, 1838.

Dickens, Charles. *Sketches by Boz: Illustrative of Every-Day Life and Every-Day People.* London: Chapman & Hall, 1903.

"Do Children Need Sex Roles?" *Newsweek,* June 10, 1974.

"Does a Boy Have the Right to Be Effeminate?" *Psychology Today,* April 1979.

Ellison, Jesse. "My Parents' Failed Experiment in Gender Neutrality." *Newsweek,* March 23, 2010.

"Fashions: Baby's Clothes." *Time,* November 17, 1927.

Fausto-Sterling, Anne, Karl Lauzanne, Amanda Derryck, Ellen Lee, Melanie Blackless, and Anthony Charuvastra. "How Sexually Dimorphic Are We? Review and Synthesis." *American Journal of Human Biology* 12 (2000): 151–66.

Fine, Cordelia. *Delusions of Gender: How Our Minds, Society, and Neurosexism Create Difference.* New York: W. W. Norton, 2010.

Flugel, John Carl. *The Psychology of Clothes.* London: Hogarth Press, 1930.

Gibralter, Marshall. "Reconsidering Dresses: If Dresses Are Dead, Then Why Are They Selling?" *Earnshaw's Infants, Girls and Boys Wear Review,* April 1973.

Grant, Julia. "A 'Real Boy' and Not a Sissy: Gender, Childhood, and Masculinity, 1890–1940." *Journal of Social History* 37, no. 4 (2004): 829–51.

Griffith, John Price. *The Care of the Baby.* 4th ed. Philadelphia: W. B. Saunders, 1908.

Hall, G. Stanley. "The Feminist in Science." *Independent,* March 22, 1906.

———. "How and When to Be Frank with Boys." *Ladies' Home Journal,* September 1907.

———. "New Lights on Childhood." *Youth's Companion,* October 28, 1915.

Harrington, Henry F. "The Southerner's Daughter." *Godey's Magazine and Lady's Book,* January 1842.

Harris, Judith Rich. "Where Is the Child's Environment? A Group Socialization Theory of Development." *Psychological Review* 102, no. 3 (1995): 458–89.

Hayes, Joseph M., and N. Ray Hiner, eds. *American Childhood: A Research Guide and Historical Handbook.* Westport, Conn.: Greenwood Press, 1985.

Heininger, Mary Lynn Stevens. *A Century of Childhood, 1820–1920.* Rochester, N.Y.: Margaret Woodbury Strong Museum, 1984.

Helgoe, Laurie A., and Barron M. Helgoe. *The Complete Idiot's Guide to Raising Boys.* New York: Alpha Books, 2008.

"Holiday Forecast." *Earnshaw's Infants, Girls and Boys Wear Review,* August 1968.

"The Home Club." *Outlook,* February 15, 1896.

Hooper, Emma M. "Hints on Home Dressmaking." *Ladies' Home Journal,* January, September, and November 1893.

Hurlbert, Anya C., and Yazhu Ling. "Biological Components of Sex Differences in Color Preference." *Current Biology* 17, no. 16 (August 21, 2007): R623–R625.

"Infants' Clothing." *Delineator,* July 1896.

"It Was Babies' Day." *New York Times,* October 5, 1890, sec. 2.

Javitt, Gail H. "Pink or Blue? The Need for Regulation Is Black and White." *Fertility and Sterility* 86, no. 1 (July 2006): 13–15.

Jensen, Juanita Leisch. "The Economics of Intended Re-use: A Presentation in Which the Author Reveals How to Tell the Boys from the Girls, Identifies Work Garments, Explains Auction Prices, and Solves Many Other Mysteries of the Universe." Paper read at Costume Society of America Region 6 conference, Williamsburg, Va., October 2008.

Johnson, Franklin W. "The Problems of Boyhood: A Course of Ethics for Boys in the Sunday School." *Biblical World,* April 1914.

Jordan, David Starr. *The Call of the Twentieth Century.* Boston: American Unitarian Association, 1903.

Kaiser, Susan B. "Sex Typing in Dress: A Developmental Approach." *ACPTC Proceedings,* 124. Houston: ACPTC, 1986.

Kaiser, Susan B., and Kathleen Huun. "Fashioning Innocence and Anxiety: Clothing, Gender, and Symbolic Childhood." In *Symbolic Childhood,* ed. Daniel Cook. New York: Peter Lang, 2002.

Kennedy, Pagan. *Platforms: A Microwaved Cultural Chronicle of the 1970s.* New York: St. Martin's Press, 1994.

Kett, Joseph F. "Adolescence and Youth in Nineteenth-Century America." *Journal of Interdisciplinary History* 2 (1971): 283–98.

Laskin, David, and Kathleen O'Neill. *The Little Girl Book: Everything You Need to Know to Raise a Daughter Today.* New York: Ballantine Books, 1992.

Limpert, Ann. "Is Pink the New Blue?" *Washingtonian,* August 2004.

"Little Lord Fauntleroy." *Peterson's Magazine,* February 1890.

Lo, Danica. "Video: The Denim Huggies Diaper Commercial Is Creepy and Genius: 'My Diaper Is Full of Chic! I Poo in Blue!'" http://racked.com/ archives/2010/05/26/video-the-denim-huggies-diaper-commercial-is-creepy-and-genius-my-diaper-is-full-of-chic-i-poo-in-bl.php.

Maccoby, Eleanor. *The Two Sexes: Growing Up Apart, Coming Together.* Cambridge: Belknap Press of Harvard University Press, 1998.

Maccoby, Eleanor Emmons, and Carol Nagy Jacklin. *The Psychology of Sex Differences.* Stanford: Stanford University Press, 1974.

Maurice, Arthur Bartlett. "Best Sellers of Yesterday." *Bookman,* September 1911.

McCracken, Grant. *Culture and Consumption: New Approaches to the Symbolic Character of Consumer Goods and Activities.* Bloomington: Indiana University Press, 1990.

———. *Culture and Consumption II: Markets, Meaning, and Brand Management.* Bloomington: Indiana University Press, 2005.

"Medicine: Test-Tube Baby: It's a Girl." *Time,* August 7, 1978.

Money, John, and Anke Ehrhardt. *Man & Woman, Boy & Girl.* Baltimore: Johns Hopkins University Press, 1972.

Moore, Sheila, and Roon Frost. *The Little Boy Book: A Guide to the First Eight Years.* New York: Ballantine Books, 1986.

"Mrs. Deland's *Awakening of Helena Richie.*" *Congregationalist and Christian World,* July 28, 1906.

"A New Day Dawning at Sears." *Earnshaw's Infants, Girls and Boys Wear Review,* February 1988.

"The Nursery." *Godey's Magazine and Lady's Book,* March 1852.

Orenstein, Peggy. *Cinderella Ate My Daughter: Dispatches from the Front Lines of the New Girlie-Girl Culture.* New York: HarperCollins, 2011.

————. "What's Wrong with Cinderella?" *New York Times Magazine,* December 24, 2006.

Paoletti, Jo B. "Ridicule and Role Models as Factors in American Men's Fashion Change, 1880–1910." *Costume* 19, no. 1 (1985): 121–31.

"Pink or Blue?" *Infants' Department,* June 1918.

Pollard, Brooke. "Huggies Crosses the Line (Video)." *Cuddlebugs,* June 29, 2010. http://cuddlebugs.onslow.org/cuddlebugs/tag/huggies-denim-diaper-commercial/.

Pollock, Linda. *Forgotten Children: Parent-Child Relations from 1500 to 1900.* Cambridge: Cambridge University Press, 1983; rept., 1996.

"The Power of a Frilly Apron: Coming of Age in Sodom and New Milford." *Psychology Today,* September 1975.

"Questions and Answers." *Vogue,* May 7, 1900.

Randolph, Althea. *A Shower of Verses.* New York: H. W. Gray, 1914.

Raphael, Murray. "How to Sell Infants and Toddler Wear." *Earnshaw's Infants, Girls and Boys Wear Review,* February 1968.

Robinson, Harriet Jane Hanson. *Loom and Spindle; or, Life among the Early Mill Girls.* New York: T. Y. Crowell, 1898.

Roosevelt, Theodore. "What Can We Expect of the American Boy." *St. Nicholas: An Illustrated Magazine for Young Folks,* May 1900.

Seavey, C., S. Katz, and S. Zalk. "Baby X: The Effect of Gender Labels on Adult Responses to Infants." *Signs* 1 (1975): 103–109.

"Selling Infants' Clothing." *Earnshaw's Infants, Girls and Boys Wear Review,* February 1973.

Simmel, Georg. "Fashion." *American Journal of Sociology* 62, no. 6 (1957): 541–58.

Steele, Valerie. "The F-Word." *Lingua Franca,* April 1991, 17–20.

Stein, Sara. *Girls & Boys: The Limits of Nonsexist Childrearing.* New York: Scribner, 1983.

Stone, George P. "Appearance and the Self." In *Human Behavior and Social Processes.* Boston: Houghton-Mifflin, 1962.

"The Theatres." *New York Times,* December 2, 1888, sec. 3.

Thwaite, Ann. *Waiting for the Party.* New York: Charles Scribner's Sons, 1974.

"The Twins, Punch and Judy." *Woman's Home Companion,* November 1923–July 1924.

"Ultrasound: Sonogram." *American Pregnancy Association,* March 2006. http://www.americanpregnancy.org/prenataltesting/ultrasound.html.

University Society. *The Child Welfare Manual: A Handbook of Child Nature and Nurture for Parents and Teachers.* Vol. 1. New York: University Society, 1916.

Veblen, Thorstein. *The Theory of the Leisure Class.* New York: Dover, 1994.

Ward, William Russ. "Our Boys." *Outlook,* December 1896.

Warwick, Edward, Henry C. Pitz, and Alexandra Wyckoff. *Early American Dress.* New York: Benjamin Blom, 1965.

Wehrle, Louise, and Jo B. Paoletti. "What Do We Wear to the Wedding Now That the Funeral Is Over?" *Dress* 16 (1990): 81–87.

"What Are Little Girls Made of? Puppy Dogs' Tails, Too." *Psychology Today,* August 1974.

Wilson, Craig. "Marlo Thomas: 'Free to Be' for You and Me, 35 Years Later." *USA Today,* October 6, 2008.

Wishy, Bernard. *Child and the Republic: The Dawn of Modern American Child Nurture.* Philadelphia: University of Pennsylvania Press, 1968.

"Woman at Home." *Godey's Magazine and Lady's Book,* January 1831.

Worrell, Estelle Ansley. *Children's Costume in America, 1607–1910.* New York: Scribner, 1980.

Wyden, Barbara. "When Both Wear the Pants." *St. Petersburg Times,* March 1, 1970.

Wyden, Peter. *Growing Up Straight: What Every Thoughtful Parent Should Know about Homosexuality.* New York: Stein and Day, 1975.

Yum Yum. "The Letter-Box." *St. Nicholas: An Illustrated Magazine for Young Folks,* June 1886.

INDEX

Page numbers in italics represent illustrations.

Jo B. Paoletti is Associate Professor of American Studies at the University of Maryland. She has spent more than thirty years researching and writing about children's clothing in America, particularly the development of gender differences. A passionate teacher, she has also published articles and book chapters on service-learning, undergraduate research, and the use of new technologies in humanities teaching and learning.